THE CAIRNGORMS

A Secret History

Patrick Baker

BIRLINN

First published in 2014 by Birlinn Ltd
West Newington House
10 Newington Road
Edinburgh
EH9 1QS

www.birlinn.co.uk

Reprinted in 2015, 2019 and 2021

ISBN: 978-1-78027-188-0

British Library Cataloguing in Publication Data
A catalogue record for this book is available from the
British Library

Typeset in Sabon at Birlinn

Printed and bound in Great Britain
by Clays Ltd, Elcograf S.p.A.

Contents

Illustrations

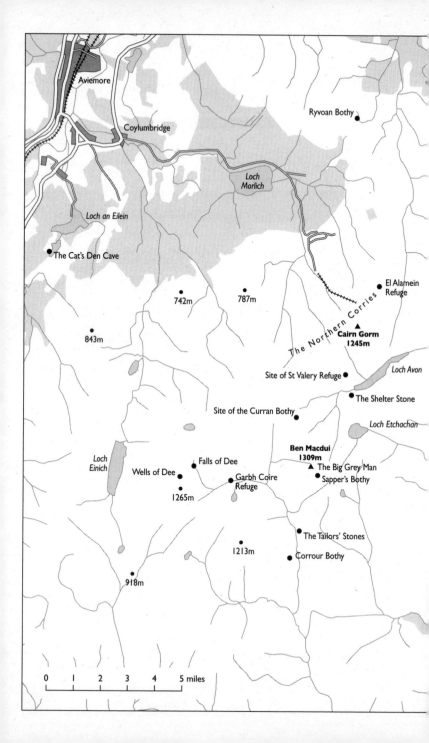

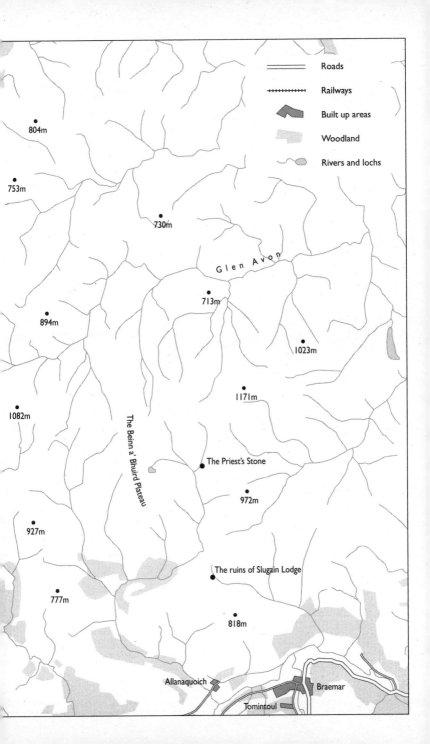

Roads

Railways

Built up areas

Woodland

Rivers and lochs

• 804m

• 753m

• 730m

G l e n   A v o n

• 713m

• 894m

• 1023m

• 1171m

• 1082m

The Beinn a' Bhuird Plateau

The Priest's Stone

• 972m

• 927m

The ruins of Slugain Lodge

• 777m

• 818m

Allanaquoich

Braemar

Tomintoul

Dedication

For my wife Jacqui, and for my children Isla, Rory and Finn, with all my love.

Secret Histories

'The exploratory urge moves every man who loves the hills.'

W. H. Murray

For a few fleeting seconds, my mind defaulted to known surroundings: to my bed at home and a drowsy feeling of safety and cosiness. The sensation quickly passed; I came to shuddering in the darkness, temporarily disorientated by the cold, but slowly remembering where I was. It was midnight on the summit of the Cairngorm plateau and I hunkered down further into my sleeping bag, suppressing a mild sense of panic about the possible onset of hypothermia and questioning the wisdom of spending the night alone at over 4,000 feet.

For almost an hour I lay awake watching the sky's patterns. Jigsaw patches of cumulus clouds scudded overhead, tesselating and decoupling from each other against the dark firmament. An icy north-westerly rolled across the night's empty spaces. It rattled through my bivouac bag, inflating, then collapsing, pockets of cold mountain air all around me. Sleep seemed impossible, and eventually a restless, nervous energy got the better of me. Tired of shivering and too cold to stay still, I left my shelter and began to tread the nightscape of the plateau.

I walked roughly eastwards following a tiny spring-fed stream whose surface glinted like molten metal. The wind gusted steadily at my back, hustling against the material of my jacket and nudging me forward with every step. On the plateau's western rim the moon drifted large and low, and ahead of me the land dipped into a shallow depression at least half a kilometre wide. Dozens of wellsprings collected there, each throwing back the moonlight like tiny droplets of mercury. Beyond the watershed, the horizon rose in a gentle incline, edging towards its uppermost point, the summit of Braeriach: the second-highest mountain in the Cairngorms and the third-highest peak in Britain.

From the abstract thoughts that accompany complete solitude, a daft, random notion entered my mind: unless, for some equally unfathomable reason, someone else was spending the night on either of the UK's two higher places, Ben Nevis or Ben Macdui, I realised that I was, at that moment, the highest human being in Britain. I was, in fact, probably higher than anyone else on the western peripheries of Europe.

For a few seconds, the thought unbalanced me, tipping me back again towards panic. What was I doing? I was dozens of kilometres and a thousand elevated metres from the nearest place of human habitation, effectively stranded until sunrise in one of the country's most inhospitable natural environments. Alone in the high-altitude darkness, the realisation of my self-enforced remoteness sent a brief, electric current pulsing through my stomach. I felt foolhardy, and a bit naive.

Suddenly my plan seemed rather ridiculous. Several months earlier, sitting at my kitchen table with the last shafts of evening sun cutting into the room, the thought of making a series of journeys to explore some of the most desolate and seldom visited parts of Britain's wildest mountain range had seemed like a good idea. What better way to find out more about a place that over the years I had become slightly obsessed with?

Back then, the practicalities of the project had hardly even registered with me. It would take a while, of course: a year perhaps, in between the commitments of work and family life; but it would be feasible, even enjoyable. They were to be adventures, unconventional mountainous escapades to places I would have never normally thought of venturing.

Now, though, at one o'clock in the morning, jogging on the spot to keep warm, on top of Britain's third-highest mountain, I couldn't help wondering if this was more than I had bargained for.

❦

I had first visited the Cairngorms when I was in my early twenties. I was on a training course for would-be mountaineers, learning the rudiments of winter hillcraft from an instructor hell-bent on leaving behind any of us who were too slow to keep up. By early afternoon we had picked our way up a steep ice bank in Coire an t-Sneachda, one of the towering, snow-encrusted Northern Corries. Perhaps it was the oxygen-depleted exertion, the rush of endorphins or the elation at finally pulling up on to the plateau edge, but I was momentarily overcome by what I then saw.

I stood breathless, staring out across a snowbound territory of ice-fields, turreted island summits and kilometres of crystalline brightness that stretched as far as my eyes could see. Then, as now, I felt an utter bewilderment at the sheer size of the Cairngorms. No other area of Britain is so immensely high over such an immensely large area. Its elevation and geographical extent make it unique: a monolithic expanse of mountainous granite landmass equivalent in size to Luxembourg and containing five of the six highest peaks in Britain.

Accordingly, it is known as a place of extremes and cruel asperities, of unparalleled topographical and altitudinal circumstance. Snow falls here in every month of the year and lies permanently in its coldest recesses. Gales regularly batter the plateau with such ferocity that windspeeds have reached over 170mph. Temperatures and conditions are subarctic in their severity and fatalities are recorded here regularly.

But beyond its immediate first impressions, its hostile bleakness and prodigious expanse, an alternative identity of the range also exists. It is a corresponding but often concealed character, described by the modernist poet and novelist Nan Shepherd, as the 'living mountain', in her unashamedly eulogistic book of the same name. For like all wild places, the Cairngorms harbour hidden narratives: geological, animal and human – past events and contemporary passages which are rarely acknowledged in the same way as urban and industrialised histories, but are nonetheless evidenced within the landscape; if, of course, you know where to look.

It was the Cairngorms, more than any other remote or mountainous area that I knew, which seemed to retain and perpetuate these secret histories. It seemed, as well, that despite – or perhaps because of – its fearsome wildness, there were stories and mysteries here that were more potent and intriguing than anywhere else I could think of.

The journeys I hoped to make would be to explore the Cairngorms' secret histories. To search for the relics and rumours that marked the unofficial, unrecorded character of the range. Seemingly anomalous vestiges like the high-level shelters of the plateau – the refuges once used by generations of climbers, but now all but crumbling into obscurity. Elsewhere, I plotted expeditions to find the unlikeliest and most interesting of features: the skeletal remains of aircraft debris; an ancient gem mine; the cave of a local fugitive; a mysterious aristocratic settlement; ghostly apparitions; geological oddities; and a secluded, little-known ravine. I also intended to follow the natural routes of the landscape, to track the course of the River Dee, trailing its backwards slant into the tundra of the Braeriach plateau, in search of the highest river source in Britain. I even tried to deduce the most likely place to see a wildcat.

There would be no ground-breaking discoveries or grand revelations, I was sure of that. I had no real idea of what, if anything, I would find. My leads were questionable at best: a dubious collection of obscure publications, out-of-print books and unsubstantiated online chatter. At worst, they were distinctly flimsy: dimly remembered conversations, drunken anecdotes and spurious pub stories. But that, in many ways, was the point. I was looking for the *alter ego* of these hills, something of the overlooked, the obscure and the unobserved in Britain's greatest mountain wilderness.

Ghost River

'Though actually I have one small idea – I intend to walk a certain river to its source.'
Neil M. Gunn, *Highland River*.

In late July 1829, a high-pressure system situated in the Atlantic Ocean, between southern Iceland and northern Scotland, retreated south-westwards. In its wake, a chain of atmospheric events began to unfold. Cold air swept south from the Norwegian Arctic, through Scandinavia and the Baltic Sea, and by 1 August a substantial depression had begun to make its ways southwards from Iceland, gaining momentum as it travelled.

Weather conditions on land would have begun to deteriorate correspondingly, but for the people of north-east Scotland, blissfully unaware of the extraordinary meteorological changes that were taking place at sea, daily life continued as normal. Little could anyone have known that within days, one of the most cataclysmic natural events ever recorded in Britain would take place.

On 3 August 1829 the full force of the Atlantic depression eventually reached mainland Scotland. As the cold weather systems from the north collided with existing cyclonic systems from the south, a massive, unstable air mass formed, unleashing torrential rain as it passed slowly across the uplands of the Moray Firth and the Grampian Mountains. The result was a catastrophic flood of Biblical proportions.

The 'Muckle Spate', literally meaning 'large flood', of 1829 remains historically unparalleled in its destructive force. Thousands of people across the northeast of Scotland were rendered destitute by the rising water. Farms were swept away and vast tracts of fertile land were ruined. In one district alone, thirteen bridges and three sawmills were destroyed by the swollen rivers. Elsewhere, roads were inundated and whole communities left stranded. Eight people lost their lives and many more had their livelihoods obliterated. Within a matter of hours, the rivers that had been the lifeblood of the region had become the conduits of its destruction.

It was hardly surprising. The rivers of north-east Scotland possess a latent ferocity. They are mountain rivers, capable of rapid and violent transformation, falling further and faster than anywhere else in the country: rivers such as the Spey and the Avon whose waters rise disparately in the Cairngorm and Monadhliath mountains; and the River Dee whose headwaters on top of the Braeriach plateau have the highest and most enigmatic river source in Britain.

I once idly traced the backwards course of the River Dee, letting my finger run gradually northwards and upwards along its representation on the Ordnance Survey map. The river's depiction on the map steadily changed the further my finger moved against its downward flow, tapering from fat blue curves, looping and bending across the map, through green forestry and salmon-pink villages, to a narrow line, split thinner and thinner at each V-shaped confluence.

Eventually the river became a slender cobalt filament surrounded by the compressed orange of merging contour lines and the black symbolism of cliffs. I followed the blue strand on the map until it could divide no further, to the river's ultimate source, in the middle of the Cairngorm Mountains.

A few small blue circles were scattered at the place where my finger finally rested, too small to be lochans or tarns, but large enough to make it onto the map. Next to them was a name in the same blue typeface, 'The Wells of Dee'. I was immediately intrigued. Every other river that I could see on the map eventually subdivided backwards into obscurity. The River Dee was different. I was able to follow its headwaters back to one of the highest points on the map.

Not only that, its source had a name. It made the starting point of the river seem almost official. The inclusion of the triangle of blue circles on the map hinted at a sense of permanence, a geographical feature present year after year, a constant supply of water. But from where? There was no higher ground from which rainwater could drain, and to my knowledge the plateau summit was a hard, boulder-strewn landscape, not a marshland. The 'Wells' had to be wellsprings, the source of the river flowing from within the very mountain itself.

Years later, there now seemed to be an exploratory logic to walking the course I had once plotted with my finger. Travelling upstream, back to the source of the Dee, meant moving within the landscape, and understanding something of the water's anarchic progression to lower ground. It would also be an unravelling of the river, witnessing its life-history unfolding in reverse.

The Linn of Dee is the furthest place upstream on the River Dee that you can reach by public road. The Linn, from the Gaelic meaning a pool or a cascade of water, is a 300-metre-long chasm cleaved deep into the bedrock where the Dee suddenly converges from a broad-spanning river to a raging torrent just a couple of metres wide. It is spectacular, but concealed until you are close by, hidden amongst thick stands of larch and lodgepole pine. It was dusk when I arrived and the place was deserted. The air was still warm and smelt strongly of pine resin.

A small stone bridge spanned the gorge, arching above a narrow channel of spluttering white-water. The bridge's wooden predecessor was one of first significant victims of the Muckle Spate, pulled apart despite being ten metres above the water. Other bridges further downstream suffered similar fates during the deluge. Not even the engineering prowess of Thomas Telford could have foreseen the destructive power of the 1829 flood. His huge, newly-built stone bridge at Ballater was completely dismantled by the rising waters.

I peered down into the gorge, leaning over the cliff edge, hearing the water before I could see it. On the underside of the bridge the Dee fell in a series of cascades. Recesses had been carved into the rocks in wide curves and scoops that suggested dramatic movement and indicated much higher water levels.

Remarkably the Linn had once been challenged, and tamed. In an act of incredible athleticism but utter recklessness, the celebrated English climber, John Menlove Edwards, swam the length of the falls in 1935. The river was in full spate at the time, but Edwards astonishingly survived the feat and later went on to be at the forefront of British climbing in the 1930s and '40s, pioneering many routes previously thought of as unclimbable. Edwards's life story was not a happy one, though. The apparently self-destructive compulsion that led him to swim the Linn of Dee perhaps underpinned his complex, troubled personality. He later committed suicide in 1958.

Twilight gathered quickly. The sky was cloudless and shifting from blue to purple. I walked westwards, leaving the forestry and moving out into the grassy moorland of Glen Dee, keen to cover as much ground as possible before full darkness. My route ran parallel with the river, separated from it by a floodplain that held some of the largest Scots pines I had ever seen. The trees were colossal and stately: russet-tinged branches and huge blue-green crowns, each with its own wide circumference of territory.

My eyes began to refocus as I walked, adjusting to the grainy half-light. I caught outlines and patterns instead of close detail. Then, several kilometres in, I noticed something partially covered amongst the heather: linear profiles that in their configuration and placement somehow seemed out of place. The track swung close to the shapes, and I paced across the moorland to see them.

I found rows of small boulders, linked at right angles and half hidden by moss and turf that had grafted on top of them: the architectural footprints of a long-deserted building. This was once a homestead, a place of family life and part of a succession of dwellings scattered along the plains of the Dee: to the south of the river, the farmsteads of Dalvor and Dubrach; to the north, Tonnagaoithe and the ruins of Tomnamoine in which I stood. In the darkness, the building's remains seemed poignant, ghostly: distinct archaeological signifiers of one of the most shameful periods of social upheaval in Scotland's history.

By the early nineteenth century the agricultural landscape of Scotland was rapidly changing. Influenced in part by the erosion of the clan system and the gradual agrarian change that had already occurred in England, farming communities that had lived for centuries in Glen Dee and across the Highlands of Scotland swiftly began to vanish. The landowners and large estates of Highland Scotland no longer believed their tenant farmers represented a commercially viable proposition. The old systems of croft and enclosure were rapidly beginning to disappear.

Wholesale clearances took place, swiftly and efficiently depopulating the Highland landscape. Communities were comprehensively eradicated; tens of thousands were removed from their homes by systematic violence and deception. Men, women and children faced starvation, destitution and death as the land they had worked for generations was given up to the rearing of sheep, and in the case of Glen Dee, the servicing of wealthy sporting parties.

There is little direct evidence to suggest that the tenants of Glen Dee experienced the same cruel regimes of clearance witnessed in other parts of Scotland. Instead, the eviction of the glen's farmsteads appears to have happened relatively gradually.

The first two settlements of Tomnagaoithe and Dalvorar to be cleared in 1829 could also have been prompted in no small part by the events of the Muckle Spate.

Sir Thomas Dick Lauder's meticulous chronicle of the floods details the effects of the River Dee's rising flood waters on some of the inhabitants of Glen Dee, suggesting the impact of the flood may have simply rendered the land unusable for agricultural use:

The river surrounded the house on the night of the 3rd, with so much rapidity, that the husband, the wife and seven or eight children, had hardly time to escape by wading; and they were compelled to trudge through the pelting and pitiless storm . . . The whole of their crop was destroyed, as well as eleven acres of arable land.

However, it is clear that by 1872, like many other parts of rural Scotland, the once thriving Glen Dee had been completely relieved of its tenant families. The area became a deer forest, its primary function the provision of land for hunting.

The Clearances wrought new dimensions of loss upon Scotland. There was of course the immediate physical loss of communities, occupations and lives, but also a less tangible sense of sacrifice. It was a forfeiture not immediately obvious in the shuffling demographics or huddled masses crowding boats set for the New World. As the people left the land and the glens fell silent, an intimate human connection with the landscape of Scotland was irrevocably severed. The population had shifted: a full-scale exodus from the agrarian to the industrial, from the rural to the urban, and in the act the ancient associations with the land were abruptly halted.

In Glen Dee, evidence of centuries of human habitation still remains, in shapes and patterns embossed on the landscape: the serpentine track of the ancient droving route, the geometric outlines of ruined townships and the shadow-lines of partitioned fields. Most poignantly, though, the human legacy exists on the map, in the naming of each intricate landmark and noteworthy geographic feature.

The landscape of Glen Dee simultaneously took form and became informed by its inhabitants, its features christened in usage. Likewise, the link with the land was to be reciprocated. People took the names of the places they were closely connected with, either through birth or enduring occupation. The land and the people came full circle, finding a union of identity between place and person; none more so, perhaps, than the most famous inhabitant of the glen, Peter Grant, who was known simply as 'The Auld Dubrach'.

Grant was born during a time in Scottish and British history when the bonds of land, kinship and religion were at their most fervently disputed. A year after his birth at the croft of Dubrach, less than a kilometre from the Linn of Dee, a series of skirmishes between forces loyal to the deposed Stuart monarchy and the Hanoverian government resulted in the second Jacobite uprising of 1715 (the first was in 1689), led ostensibly by the 22nd Earl of Mar in a gathering of the clans at Braemar, just a few kilometres downriver from the Dubrach farmstead.

This rebellion failed in its aim of installing the only legitimate son of James VII and II to the throne. The Jacobite revolt was roundly quelled, with its leaders fleeing to France. Attempts were made by the government forces to further subdue Jacobite uprisings in the Highlands, with the reinforcement of military garrisons at Fort William, Fort Augustus, Ruthven and Inversnaid. General Wade raised an independent militia, the Black Watch, based in the Highlands to deter crime and stifle revolt, and constructed a network of roads for the rapid mobilisation of his troops.

But the Hanoverian government's attempts to suppress the Jacobite insurgencies succeeded only partially. Fierce regional loyalties and the traditions of the clan system in the Highlands proved a fertile breeding ground for the Jacobite cause. Glen Dee and the Braemar area, in particular, largely remained rebel country, and by the age of thirty-one, Peter Grant, son of the Dubrach crofter, was bearing arms for the Stuart cause in the second Jacobite uprising of 1745.

Grant fought in the Monaltrie's and Balmoral Regiment of the Jacobite army as a Sergeant Major. He saw notable action in the Jacobite victory at the Battle of Prestonpans, where the Hanoverian army was thoroughly routed by Jacobite forces able to gain tactical advantage through a close familiarity with the battlefield terrain. His armed revolt ended, however, along with that of every other Jacobite soldier, at the Battle of Culloden, the last pitched battle on British soil. Grant survived the carnage of Culloden, but was taken prisoner and incarcerated in Carlisle Castle.

Incredibly, though, Grant not only succeeded in avoiding the likely fates of execution or deportation, but also managed to escape. He became a fugitive, his instincts leading him northwards, back to the safety of the Highlands.

Although no actual account exists of Grant's journey back to his native lands it is safe to assume the route would have been fraught with hardship and danger. Penniless and with a bounty on his head, he crossed the countryside of Scotland, evading capture by roaming bands of Hanoverian troops.

In the years after the war, Grant gradually managed to regain a semblance of normality. He was able to return, undetected by government forces, to his former life as a tailor. He later also married Mary Cummings, a woman from the Braemar area, and they had two children. Grant lived the rest of his life in peace, and, so the story goes, in relative anonymity until 1820.

Seventy-five years after the second Jacobite uprising, two wealthy gentlemen encountered Peter Grant on a hillside in Glen Lethnot. The 'Auld Dubrach', as he had then become known, took them back to his cottage and regaled them with his exploits in the Jacobite army, even demonstrating how to wield a broadsword. So impressed were the men at discovering a survivor of the Battle of Culloden and veteran of the Jacobite rebellion, they organised a petition for Grant to live out the rest of his days in a modicum of comfort. Shortly afterwards, Grant received a lifetime pension and was presented to King George IV on his visit to Edinburgh.

The Auld Dubrach died at the astoundingly old age of 110 years – his passing marking an historical watershed: a farewell not only to the claims for a Stuart monarchy, but a clear division between two epochs, a turning away from the old allegiances to land and clanship and an inexorable shift towards the compelling new forces of industrialisation, urban expansion and the awfulness of the Clearances. Peter Grant was buried in Braemar churchyard, his grave only a few miles east of his birthplace in the Dubrach croft.

———

My plan had been to travel as close to the river as I could, shadowing its twists and turns all the way to the Wells of Dee. By the next morning, however, the task had soon become too difficult. I struggled over every metre,

wading through knee-high knots of heather and slipping into pockets of thick, liquid peat. Abandoning the
attempt, I tramped the ancient pathway of the glen: the
centuries-old drovers' route that ran parallel to the river
and headed north towards the Lairig Ghru.

For two hours as I followed the rise and fall of the
undulating track, the glen hummed with a constant movement: meadow pipits and small brown butterflies flitted
above the heather and midges swarmed in tiny clouds
whenever the breeze dropped. At ground level, countless numbers of frogs sprang from the undergrowth and
spiders scuttled across boulders. Deeper into the glen, I
spotted two deer by the river's edge: a hind and her calf.
The pair moved in perfect synchronism until they sensed
my presence. They held a motionless stance for almost a
minute, kestrel-red against the bright green grass, sniffing
the air.

I had walked the Lairig Ghru several times before.
Each time, I had made the trek from north to south –
Speyside to Deeside. To arrive from the south however,
wandering upstream, was to witness the full panoramic
sweep of the valley: the deep glacial trench of the Lairig
Ghru and its kilometre-wide opening in the plateau. At
the southern end of the glen reared the Devil's Point, the
imposing gatekeeper mountain that marked the entrance
to the Lairig Ghru.

It was here that the river temporarily and unexpectedly
widened, suddenly bloated by the inflow of water from
the Geusachan Burn. It became surrounded by mosaics of
dark, swampy pools in a large delta of soft, yielding peat
bog. Even during the full heat of summer this was difficult terrain, almost impossible to move across. The land
here retained a perpetual dampness, a permanent state of

moisture locked within layers of sphagnum mosses and absorbed deeply within thick deposits of peat. No flora of any great size could grow here. The vast expanse of blanket bog was too sodden and leached with acidity.

There were however, vestiges of the ecosystems that had once dominated the glen, exposed occasionally in cross-sections of the eroded peat or glimpsed in the wash of burns: petrified tree stumps and marble-smooth roots of the ancient pines. These were the genetic ancestors of the giant Scots pines I had seen at the start of the glen. They were frozen in their final state, preserved in what the poet Seamus Heaney described as the 'kind, black butter' of the bogland, most still unseen beneath the surface of the peat hags, interred for kilometres all around me in a huge arboreal graveyard.

By early afternoon I had reached the headwall of the valley. The established track climbed towards the top of the pass but I cut left, stumbling steeply uphill over thick heather and ankle-twisting boulders. There was nowhere else in the British Isles where I could have been surrounded by greater height. Encircling the skyline above me were four of the five highest mountains in the country.

I headed north-west, gaining height as I tracked the upward slant of the Allt a' Gharbh-choire. This was the last stretch of the Dee I would trail, and its first significant tributary: a wild, free-falling cataract, spilling down the hillside in hasty cascades.

A third of the way up, I caught sight of a low structure. Blending in colour and texture against the slopes of the opposing hillside, it was barely visible at first. It was marked on the map as Garbh Coire Bothy, a formation of rounded, loaf-shaped boulders stacked in a teetering, ramshackle mound barely six-feet high by six-feet wide.

The shelter had a strangely contradictory poise: curiously melded with the landscape yet conspicuously at odds with the wildness of its surroundings; simultaneously primitive, yet inviting and homely. From the outside it looked creaturely and snug, like some Tolkien-esque hobbit lair. I crossed the burn to see it, rooting each step solidly against the strength of the down-flowing current.

The entrance was a tiny Alice-in-Wonderland-style door, hinged in a gap in the boulders; far too small for me to enter without crouching down low – hobbit-sized, in fact. Inside, the air was cold and damp like a cellar. It was only just possible to stand fully upright. This was no bothy. It was a shelter of the most basic kind, a refuge built by climbers for climbers.

A rusting apex frame formed the internal support with sack cloths and plastic sheeting lining the inner walls. Draught-funnelling holes had been plugged with an assortment of improvised insulation materials: expanding filler foam, newspaper, food-wrappers and a sock. I tried to imagine spending the night there. It would, I presume, accommodate two people with significant discomfort and, if needs be, four in complete adversity.

A faint path led upwards from the refuge, heading towards the two giant escarpments at the head of An Garbh Choire: the scallop-shaped corries of Garbh Choire Mor and Garbh Choire Dhaidh. It was a long walk for climbers to make to the start of their routes, an hour or more, I guessed, in full winter conditions. But this was some of the most isolated and committing climbing to be experienced in the Cairngorms.

The northeast face of Garbh Choire Mor collects and retains more snow than anywhere else in Britain. Huge quantities are blown from the surface of the plateau, emptying over the cliff-face in wind-driven torrents and deposited in deep slabs at the base of the corrie. In the later stages of winter, colossal cornices also form here on the plateau rim, protruding deceptively above the vertical drops, deadly balconies of friable snow.

Such is the amount of snow that collects in Garbh Choire Mor and the nature of its sheltered position that snow can often be found here at any time of the year. This is normally a place of continual snow. Yet, in an augury of shifting environmental conditions, these year-long snow packs have been disappearing. During the last century the snow only completely melted on three occasions. In the first decade alone of the twenty-first century, the thaw had already happened twice.

In the upper reaches of An Garbh Choire, the stream split into two smaller, feeder burns draining down from each of the corries. I stayed with the right-hand division as it sloshed meekly down from the Garbh Choire Dhaidh corrie, and I entered into a more mineral realm. Plant-life and groundcover were replaced by scree-runs and rock falls, the greens and browns of the lower valley giving way to monochrome greys and the glinting of quartz.

Ascending into the corrie felt like accessing a secret room. The area opened out into a large area of flat ground, perched high above the valley like a mezzanine floor, concealed within the wider architecture of the mountain. Boulder-strewn and bordered by a cirque of broken granite slopes, the corrie felt utterly remote. At the far side, carving down the centre of the corrie wall, the Falls of Dee descended from the plateau in a 60-metre ribbon of white-water. It was here, in 1810, that the first climb ever recorded in the Cairngorms took place: a Church of Scotland minister, the Reverend George Skene Keith, made a daring scramble on the steep rib of exposed granite and grass that ran adjacent to the waterfall.

I chose not to follow this precarious route. Instead, at the corrie's eastern rim I found an alternative entrance onto the plateau. The barbed skyline of the cliff edge rounded to a steep, scree-covered slope that slid beneath me in clattering footfalls of rock. I summited near the peak of Braeriach, and then circled back across the plateau in search of the Dee. A stiff breeze angled in from the west and, on the stripped-back surface of the plateau, moss campion grew in dense clumps of pinks and greens, as soft and bouncy as pin-cushions. Tiny springs leached from the granular soil, bubbling upwards in shallow puddles of clear water.

Ahead of me, half a kilometre in the distance, silhouetted against the late afternoon sun, I saw the outline of a large deer herd. Within minutes, three of the herd broke ranks and cantered towards me, their shape and pelts becoming more apparent: long spindly limbs and brindled coats. I had read about this herd, they were reindeer that had been introduced, or more precisely reintroduced, to Scotland in 1952 by a Swedish reindeer herder, Mikel Utsi. The deer now roamed freely across the tundra of the Braeriach plateau, perfectly suited to the cold conditions and high, open spaces. The rest of herd soon wandered down, thirty or forty in total, gathering around me, inquisitive and friendly, sniffing at my rucksack as I moved among them.

I stayed with the most prominent flow of water as it retreated back into the plateau. The small stream soon fissured into a meshwork of even smaller streams, each reducing and eventually disappearing into the coarse soil. These watery tendrils, I realised, were the Wells of Dee. There was no one definitive start point, no single place of derivation; I was standing amidst the assorted well-springs of the River Dee, the highest river source in the British Isles.

I quickly explored each spring in turn. Most appeared just to seep out through the sandy ground, filtering up into small patches of sodden ground, then trickling downwards to form tiny rivulets and conjoining burns. Only the largest of the springs was different; it issued forth from a wide circular crater, recessed deeply into the surrounding landscape, ten feet or more in diameter and filled with lime green mosses and long grass. The water pooled inside the hollow and formed a ready-made stream, at least a foot wide, fully formed and utterly transparent.

In her extraordinary 1977 character study of the Cairngorms, *The Living Mountain*, Nan Shepherd writes in beguiled tones about the riverhead. 'It lies like a broad leaf veined with watercourses,' Shepherd wrote. 'Astonishingly, up here at 4000 feet, it is already a considerable stream. The immense leaf that it drains is bare, surfaced with stones, gravel, sometimes sand and in places moss and grass grow on it . . . Like all profound mysteries, it is so simple it frightens me. It wells from the rock, and flows away. For unnumbered years it has welled from the rock, and flowed away. It does nothing, absolutely nothing but be itself.'

It was true; there was an intriguing permanence to the Wells. The continuous murmuring and surfacing of water within each spring marked an ever-changing, but ceaseless renewal. It was a process which made everything else in the landscape, by comparison, seem ephemeral and transitory. I thought back to the deserted townships of the previous night; to the flitting buzz of life I had witnessed in the glen earlier that day; to the remnant pines; and the forest buried beneath the peat bog.

I thought also about the floods of the Muckle Spate, the sudden fulfilment of the river's mountain-bred potential and how, at some point in the future, this would one day happen again.

—

The reindeer eventually moved on and the sun dipped below the horizon. As the temperature dropped and the wind increased, I climbed inside my bivouac bag, grateful for the shelter and the rest. I spent a cold, fitful night on the tundra and woke at first light to a silver-grey dawn.

I left for home, following the rim of the plateau eastwards, reaching the top of Cairn Toul just after six o'clock in the morning. The cloudbase had descended, cloaking the upper landscape in mist. From the summit cairn, I dropped south-west on a compass bearing, holding a course next to the cliffs and moving over rain-slickened boulders. In the breaks in the cloud, I was able to make out the glen far below. I saw the River Dee, appearing and disappearing through the fragmenting mist: dark and hard-edged, ghosting in and out of view.

Landseer's Bothy

'Sometimes I rambled to pine groves, standing like temples, or like fleets at sea, full-rigged, with wavy boughs, and rippling with light.'
Henry David Thoreau, *Walden*.

Glen Feshie lies at the western edge of the Cairngorm massif, a slender strand of forestry and riverbed that marks a geological and notional boundary. A perimeter region hinged in the margin of two landscapes. On one side, the gradual descent towards a cultivated land – worked, humanised and eventually tamed. On the other, the rising mountainous enormity of the high plateau. It was here, in the wild peripheries of the range, at the limits of permanent human habitation, that a strange encampment had once been created: a Highland Arcadia and a place of refuge, a captivating in-between world and shelter in the wildwoods.

In the early 1830s, Georgina Russell, the sixth Duchess of Bedford and one of the wealthiest women in the country, was seeking sanctuary. The preceding decade had been fraught. The health of her elderly husband had deteriorated significantly, her large extended family had been engaged in series of acrimonious quarrels and rumours abounded in polite society about her extra-marital activities.

The Duchess turned to the Scottish Highlands to provide her with an emotional and physical safe-haven. She leased Doune House, a stately home situated in the heart of the millennia-old woodland of Rothiemurchus. The house had a significant appeal to the Duchess. Not only was it close to her mother's home of Kinrara, the place of some of her happiest childhood memories, it was also a world away from her stifling, stately existence in England.

Despite the remote location of her Highland home, the Duchess appeared to have craved an even greater isolation. Several kilometres further south of the Doune, in the forested upper reaches of Glen Feshie, the Duchess ordered the construction of a set of secluded hideaways: faux-rustic refuges hidden amongst the ancient pines, where she would stay for weeks on end living out a contrived but simple lifestyle, far removed from the privileges that her aristocratic position granted her, yet mercifully free from its public scrutiny. It was here, during her stays at the Glen Feshie huts, distanced from the suspicions of her husband and the prying eyes of Georgian society, that she conducted a love affair: a scandalous tryst with a young artist over twenty years her junior.

The artist was Edwin Landseer, the possessor of a phenomenal but mercurial talent: one of the most celebrated painters of the day, whose work would eventually include the iconic image of the 'Monarch of the Glen' and the lions of Trafalgar Square, but a man racked by his own personal demons of depression and mental ill-heath.

The couple had first met when Landseer was only eighteen and already fêted as a promising young artist. The Duke of Bedford became Landseer's first major patron. In his time spent in the Bedford household a mutual but concealed attraction developed between Landseer and the Duchess. Unbeknown to the Duke, by the time he first commissioned Landseer to paint his wife's portrait, it was probable the Duchess and the artist were already lovers.

In a coincidence of themes, I travelled to this transitional part of the Cairngorms during nature's own turning point, the vernal equinox. Straddling the cold remnant weather of a hard winter and the tilt into the long hours of summer, I was eager to discover what, if anything, remained of the Duchess's secretive forest boltholes.

I had heard of a bothy deep within the most wooded section of the glen that I would head to: a basic shelter with access to the Munros of Sgor Gaoith and Mullach Clach a' Bhlair, as well as some of the best shooting areas on the Feshie Estate. The Ruigh-aiteachain bothy's connection to the Duchess and her lover appeared intriguingly tangible. It was referred to by many, not by its Gaelic name, but by a telling historical soubriquet: Landseer's Bothy.

———

Little is now known of the Glen Feshie huts. Their one-time presence in the glen is consigned largely to local history or the occasional, fleeting reference in guidebooks. Yet although their exact number and location still remain uncertain, it is clear they were built to a deliberate aesthetic purpose – an intentionally primitive, but consciously idealised form.

The most illuminating account of the huts comes from the letters of one of the Duchess's many society guests. The celebrated comic actor Charles James Mathews visited Glen Feshie in 1833 at the invitation of his friend Landseer. Mathews, at the time a young apprentice architect yet to achieve the fame of his later life, describes his stay with an obvious sense of wonderment:

I entered that part of the pass which is called *par excellence* 'the glen' . . . I was immediately conducted to view the habitation and certainly never saw anything so half original in conception or so perfect in execution as the whole thing. The appearance was that of an Indian settlement, consisting of one low building containing three or four bedrooms and the kitchen &c., and two smaller ones of one room each, the one being dining-room, parlour, drawing-room, and hall, and the other containing two beds for the ladies.

The construction and form of the huts would have been a crude novelty to the high-society guests. And Mathews's letters hint at a thrilling, momentary departure from the opulence of the Regency high-society. 'The buildings themselves looked like the poorest peasant's cottages. The walls made of turf and overgrown with foxglove, and the roof of untrimmed spars of birch. The apartments within corresponded perfectly with their exterior. Everything of rough unpeeled birch, except the uncovered turf walls. The fires of peat and clear-burning fir blazed away upon the ground, in short, everything bespeaking the habitation of some tasteful wood-cutter.'

While staying at the huts, visitors were also expected to participate in the fantasy of a pastoral Highland existence, donning traditional Highland garb; hunting; fishing and feasting on wild game. It was a perfectly pleasant, but entirely bogus interpretation of the actual realities of Highland life at the time.

Several pictures that exist of the huts reinforce the sense of false modesty, of comfortable slumming. Landseer's painting of the entrance of one of the buildings is revealing for the minor details it includes. The picture shows a portico constructed from spars supporting a turfed roof and decorated with antlers and a Highland targe. The exterior speaks of a simple, rustic construction yet a glimpse through the open doorway shows a more sophisticated interior – a decanter and a silver candle-stick-holder placed upon a well-finished chest of drawers.

Two further pictures of the huts, one drawn by Mathews, the other by an unnamed artist, also betray a grandeur at odds with the simplicity of a humble Highland dwelling. Both portray interiors, and each depicts a light and airy room with a high timber-vaulted ceiling and a large dining table and chairs occupying the foreground. In one of the pictures, the walls are lavishly adorned with antlers and rams' horns, there are tartan drapes and a curtained window at which an elegant young woman sits reading a book.

The Glen Feshie huts were cruelly ironic, built at a time when many similar buildings were being destroyed in the Clearances. They were an endearing but callous fraud, evidence not only of the collective indifference of the ruling aristocracy to the plight of many Highlanders, but also the embodiment of the new and boldly roman-ticised view of the Highland landscape that had been imagined by Sir Walter Scott.

In the fading years of the Enlightenment and after dec-ades of political and social turmoil during the Jacobite rebellions and the Napoleonic wars, Scott's writing rein-vented and reinvigorated notions of Scotland's culture and identity. The 'land of the mountain and the flood' had become the backdrop to an intoxicating mix of chivalric endeavour, historical heroism and scintillating romance. For the first time, the Highlands of Scotland had been gifted a new and tangible sense of reality in the public consciousness: no longer a hostile hinterland, they were a desirable landscape to be appreciated and explored.

It was almost certainly Scott's fictionalised projections of Scotland that prompted the building of the Glen Feshie huts. In turn, the huts played their part in perpetuating a Georgian, then Victorian obsession with all things Highland. Landseer, their artist in residence, became the heir apparent to Scott's romantic Highland visions. He consigned to canvas the iconic imagery of Scott's literature, inspired in no small part by the scenery he encountered during his stays in Glen Feshie.

By the early 1860s, however, the huts had fallen into ruin. The final noteworthy descriptions of the buildings are to be found in extracts from Queen Victoria's *Highland Journals*. The Queen first encountered the huts on a trip made in September 1860. The description provides not only an indication as to the huts' position in the glen but also conjures up a lamentable end to their brief existence.

> We walked on a little way to where the valley and glen widen out and where there is what they call a green 'hard' . . . where the finest fir-trees are, amidst some of the most beautiful scenery possible. Then we came upon a most lovely spot – the scene of all Landseer's glory – and where there is a little encampment of wooden and turf huts, built by the late Duchess of Bedford; now no longer belonging to the family, and, alas! All falling into decay – among splendid fir-trees, the mountains rising abruptly from the sides of the valley.

The second extract was written after another visit by the Queen just over a year later. The Duchess had died eight years previously and Landseer, although still one of nation's most famous artists, was by this stage, largely debilitated by mental instability. Queen Victoria was undoubtedly moved by the poignancy of the derelict huts and the beauty of their setting.

> The huts, surrounded by magnificent fir-trees, and by quantities of juniper-bushes, looked lovelier than ever; and we gazed with sorrow at their utter ruin. I felt what a delightful little encampment it must have been, and how enchanting to live in such a spot as this beautiful solitary wood in a glen, surrounded by the high hills.

Curiously, the huts remained intact enough for the Queen to enter one of them. In the ruined building she came across a legacy of Landseer's time there – an elaborate fresco of stags he had painted on the chimney breast.

Almost thirty years after their construction and many years after their habitation, the neglected huts must have looked strangely memorial in appearance; abandoned, overgrown and incongruous with their surroundings. Decaying epitaphs for a long-lost love affair.

—

In the days before my visit, I began to picture Glen Feshie as an island. A place surrounded, contained. Bounded to the west by the River Feshie's rapids, bordered to the east by the steep swell of the plateau and cut off from the south by vast tracts of moorland wilderness. I entered from the north, crossing the fourth of its natural boundaries.

The Allt Garbhlach drains from the high ground of the Moine Mhor – the 'Great Moss' of the Cairngorm plateau. The stream descends steeply from the hillside, cutting a tight chicane through sheer-sided slopes, before straightening and widening at its lower reaches. Season-shifting storms had been building all week and the stream churned fast through its boulder eddies. I waded thigh-deep through the snow-melt waters, stepping sideways across the currents in a clumsy crab-like shuffle.

The forestry began at the stream bank. A dark screen of plantation conifers, regimented and orderly, condensed the daylight to a premature dusk. Silence reverberated within: little, if any, wildlife chooses to exist in such dense forms of monoculture. The natural processes of real forests are forgotten. Rhythms of life and death, of regeneration and decay are spurned. Growth is fast, multiple and synchronised, leaching the soil and blocking out the sun in a place of perpetual twilight. I threaded my way through the tightly spaced trunks, fracturing dry branches underfoot, each breaking with sharp, brittle snaps.

Soon the plantation unfolded and the woodland became more ancient. Daylight and bird song returned: at first the occasional, staccato trill of chaffinches, then the rapid-fire chirrups of tits, high in the canopy, and the piping calls of oystercatchers by the riverbank.

Close to where the Feshie bordered the forest edge, I spotted the ruin of an old building, now almost completely covered in a creeping, vegetative understorey. I pulled hard at the tangled undergrowth. Dusty red brick lay beneath. It was a bunker of some sort, next to which there was the concrete base of a much larger building. I guessed at a military connection. Glen Feshie and the eastern side of the Cairngorms were used extensively for training troops during the Second World War and the ruin had most probably been an army building.

From the confines of the woodland I connected with a faint path that ran alongside the river. The landscape opened up to a broad savannah of yellowing grassland scattered with stocky pines, armour-plated in bark as thick as dinosaur skin. After an hour of wandering, with several imagined sighting and false discoveries, I came across the weather-greyed remains of the Carnachuin Bridge. I had seen the bridge before in an old photograph that predated its collapse. Even then, the image showed a doubtful wooden structure. Boarded with planks, it dipped precariously in its centre as a couple of hillwalkers made their way tentatively across it.

Two signs had been fixed to a post next to the bridge. The first was a warning, cautioning against its use and acknowledging its frailty: 'If you choose to cross Carnachuin Bridge and thereby willingly accept the risks involved – we suggest that there are no more than two people at any one time'. The second sign had been placed below the first, sometime afterwards, noting the bridge's eventual demise. 'Washed away,' it read, 'in the spate of September 3rd, 2009.' All that now remained of the bridge was its imaginary span, linking the two crumbling ramparts that clutched the banks on either side of the river.

A scurrying wind brought a handful of rain as it progressed past me, south through the valley. The sky behind was a curdled grey and the late afternoon light began to dim. Once again the glen felt as it were somewhere on the edge of things, separate and somehow cut off. A twofold place of opposing significances, isolated but protected, remote but secret.

Isolation and remoteness, protection and secrecy. I knew why the huts had been built in the woods of Glen Feshie. Not the specific, detailed reasons, of course, but something closer to the deep personal motivations behind their construction: the need to escape, to reposition yourself somewhere wilder, more elemental than everyday life would permit.

It is easy to assume the desire to connect with wild places is a symptom of our modern times, a necessary counterpoint to the pressures of our increasingly urbanised lifestyles. To reach a secluded forest, walk astride a knife-edge ridge or summit a deserted peak is to realign perspectives; to become temporarily disencumbered of day-to-day concerns and be reminded of the more immediate priorities of existence. Yet the ritual of retreat, of finding refuge in wilderness, no matter how temporary or fleeting, is nothing new.

When I pictured the Glen Feshie huts being used, I tried to imagine similar moments of escape. I was aware the huts had hosted some decadent parties with wealthy guests marvelling at the primitiveness of their surroundings. But I preferred to think of the huts as being part of a more fundamental process, the same impulse to locate to wild places that even now compels the most arduous explorations or the briefest of rambles. My notion is that a retreat to somewhere wild can be a spiritually expansive experience, and perhaps, as it may have been in Landseer's case, even a redemptive one.

Glen Feshie left a permanent impression on Landseer. Shortly after his death in 1873, a large and hitherto unknown collection of his paintings was discovered. The collected works were all landscapes, dating somewhere between the 1820s and 1830s – the first two decades during which Landseer had visited Scotland. The pictures differ markedly from his commissioned and commercial work. There are no narrative scenes, no portraiture or his trademark animal imagery. Instead the paintings are oil-based sketches, clearly painted out of doors, and depict scenes Landseer would have come across on his travels in the Highlands. Unlike his more formal compositions which conform more to the ideals of the Sublime and the Romantic, these landscape paintings appear vibrant, realistic and spontaneous, accurately capturing the nuances in light and weather that are so much a part of the Highland scenery.

Amongst the Landseer landscapes, numerous images exist of Glen Feshie. The paintings all depict a large sweep of the upper glen, with the unmistakable spur of Sron Direachain and the narrow defile of Slochd Beag. One painting from the set shows the glen in turmoil. The foreground is cast in bright sunlight; heather, grasses and the pale bark of a dead tree are prominently defined by the sun's rays. Almost immediately behind, however, several other pine trees are darkened by the gathering weather. The tops of the hills in the background are merged with a black storm-cloud that consumes most of the sky, sending slanting diagonals of rain into the glen.

It is hard to look at the painting, knowing of Landseer's almost life-long battle with depression, and not to see it in symbolic terms. The turbulent, chaotic weather; the smearing rain obscuring the view; the dark foreboding clouds; and the fleeting present moment allowing a brief period of light and calm. The stormscape, however, also presents the possibility of an alternative interpretation, devoid of allegory and metaphor. Quite simply, it could be an affectionate study of somewhere that Landseer loved and where he felt at peace, no matter what its climatic moods.

Perhaps this was the reason the landscape pictures were never sold or exhibited during his lifetime. Landseer wanted them for himself. He held on to them like a photograph album. They were mementos of times when he had been surrounded by something larger, something more immediate than the inner storms that formed and reformed throughout his life.

—

The Ruigh-aiteachain bothy came into view unexpectedly. The oblique line of a gable end was suddenly obvious through the verticals of the pine trees. I had anticipated something less substantial, more tumbledown in appearance, but the building was long and squat and looked decidedly robust.

There were no windows on the side I approached, just a single door painted in a glossy version of British Racing Green. Outside a large pile of fallen timber had been stacked against the wall and an axe left cleaved into an upturned log. Screwed into to the panels of the door was a notice, welcoming the bothy's use, but advising care in the nearby hills during the stalking season.

The door was unlocked and gave way to a couple of hard shoves, jerking noisily against the interior floor. Inside was a large, low room, filled with a blue-grey light that filtered in from a small rectangular window. The place smelt strongly of pine resin and wood-smoke. A tangle of branches and assorted firewood had been left to season in the centre of the room. Hanging from the ceiling above was a collection of cutting tools: several large bow saws, a couple of hand saws and a few small axes.

At the far end of the room an elaborately glazed internal door, evidently salvaged from elsewhere, led into a second area. The back room was smaller, but more homely. There were wooden bunks against the back wall, a stove, a bench and several reclaimed office chairs with foam bursting out from the seat covers. The stone walls had been freshly whitewashed and there were candles mounted on wall sconces. By the window, on a table covered with food remains and mouse droppings, I found a visitors' book.

I sat and flicked through pages crammed with paragraphs scrawled in biro, eulogising the magic of the bothy and the glen. Occasionally there were pictures and notes left for later occupants. An entry had been logged on the day before my visit: a group passing through the glen, resting for an hour at the bothy, and clearly struck by the tranquillity of its setting.

I had naively hoped to find some sign of Landseer or the Duchess within the bothy, a mural concealed beneath cracked plaster-work or some evidence of previous habitation. Instead the bothy felt more functional than homely. It was a well-frequented estate building, maintained for its usefulness rather than any sense of preservation for posterity. The name 'Landseer's Bothy' began to seem like a dubious affectation, handed down through ancient association rather than historical fact. I unbuckled my pack and trimmed some of the branches from the firewood pile, before searching outside to replenish the timber.

As I turned the corner of the bothy, I saw what I had been looking for – a remnant of one of the Glen Feshie huts. I had practically stumbled across it in the evening's half-light: a solitary chimney stack, statuesque in appearance, approximately one metre wide and five metres in height.

It appeared fully intact, constructed from neatly shaped blocks of masonry with cleanly finished edges and well-preserved mortar. At the base there was a small opening for the firebox, and near the top I could just make out two slanting lines where the roof had joined.

I was astounded by its presence in the glen. Not just by the out-of-place strangeness of its physical form, but its defiant resilience to the elements. For over 180 years, it had been exposed to stone-shattering temperatures, mortar-crumbling rain and gale-force winds, yet remarkably it still remained, resolutely in place like a museum piece or an ancient town monument.

From the chimney's hearth I paced lengthways into the imagined building. I tried to remember the paintings of the huts, to recreate the interior in my mind's eye, but it was almost impossible to see exactly where the building began and ended. Any floorplan had been lost in the passage of time. In what I guessed was the centre of what would have been the main living area I came across a recent campfire. With such a large area in which to camp nearby, someone had chosen here. It was as if the presence of the chimney and the notion of a space once occupied still conferred a sense of shelter, of protection, long after the physical building had gone.

I decided to find an elevated view. From height, I reasoned, I would be able to see more clearly any outline the building had marked on the land: its archaeological ghost-print. On the steep hillside behind the bothy I found a faint path that led quickly upwards through a briar of small pines and ragged, over-sized juniper bushes. After half an hour I was above the tree-line, in a scrub of thick heather and snow patches. The evening sky was two-tone: dark gold, behind plum-coloured clouds. I sat and watched a storm approaching from the north: diagonal blades of rain careering south, carving through the concave opening of the glen. It reminded me of Landseer's stormscape.

The bothy and the chimney stack were both visible as I climbed – tiny, structural features, oddly discernible amidst the wide spacing of trees. I was unable to see any other buildings or hidden shapes in the landscape; no spectral impressions of the settlement or fragmentary ruins. Instead, I was offered a cartographer's impression of the glen. An aerial view of its geography: a deep, elongated glacial trough, running south to north and curving at its upper end in a sickle-shaped bend.

The River Feshie came into view at the head of the glen, curling beneath the steep slopes of Sron Direachain, then dividing into multiple, sifting channels as it passed directly below me. From above, the river's flow looked frayed and weakened, unpicked and loosened like plaits of an old rope, only to then be spliced back together as a single river at the narrowing of the floodplain.

The Feshie lays claim to be one of the most dynamic river systems in the British Isles. Meandering patterns have developed in its fast flowing waters: improbable crooks and kinks and elaborate twists and turns. The process and patterns are self-perpetuating. Erosion occurring on the outside of bends pulls loose the alluvial deposits. Gravel, sand and soil are transported further downstream, creating callouses of new terrain, overlapping on the inside of bends, redirecting flow and exaggerating curvature. Each significant spate enhances the processes of transfiguration yet further: depletion and repletion, removal and endowment.

The network of interconnecting channels I could see was the result of the river 'braiding'. A phenomenon caused by frequent movement in the highly transient riverbed. In tiny but compound actions of resettlement, hundreds of tonnes of gravel had shifted to form bars of higher ground, augmented in time by further deposits to create small continents in the river. There were islands, sometimes half a kilometre long and wide enough to hold small copses of pines and tidemarks of driftwood.

I left for the bothy with the first of the storm clouds raking above me. As I walked I startled a grouse from its heather roost. It flew from almost beneath my feet, spluttering an alarm call that sounded like the failed starting of an outboard motor. The bird flapped furiously for several seconds, then banked gracefully, its shape momentarily silhouetted against the darkening sky.

———

It rained throughout the night, a constant percussion of white noise on the corrugated roof of the bothy as I drifted in and out of sleep. The storm continued into the morning as I made my way south towards the final, upper section of the glen. Marauding squalls pushed noisily past me, hurling pellets of rain that felt like shingle being thrown at my back. The grass had become sodden and on the hillsides waterfalls churned to swollen cascades of a pure, oxygenated white. I worried vaguely about the condition of the Allt Garbhlach and my ability to return safely across it, but I was keen to explore further.

I followed the markings of a rough vehicle track as it led into a narrowing stretch of land enclosed between the torrential river and the steep forested slopes, for two kilometres until the Feshie began to bend and the only available ground was a slender path that rose on a bank high above the river.

Evidence of previous storms was everywhere. Landslides and erosions from flash floods had ripped open gashes of loose, crystalline soil. One landslip I passed was enormous, at least three metres wide and extending upwards through the forest for over fifteen metres. Inside the concave opening of earth were two fallen pine trees, wedged diagonally with their root boles exposed. I edged carefully across the incline of fast-moving soil, digging my fingertips into the bank and sending small runnels of gravel and rocks tumbling into the water below.

As I rounded the river-bend I entered a small wooded canyon, deeply shaded in a soft green light. It was a landscape of completely unexpected proportions, feeling much deeper than it was wide and flanked on either side by sheer slopes of rock and scree-fall. Moss grew everywhere, carpeting the ground and furring tree trunks in a velvety pelt. Through the forest canopy I was able to see the upper rim of the canyon, a jagged outline of sawtooth crags and teetering boulders. As I scanned the uppermost levels of the rock-face, something else caught my eye. Among the crimps and folds of granite were two dark vertical slots – caves, human-sized recesses that appeared to retreat some distance back into the crags and which looked virtually impossible to reach without climbing equipment.

Accessing them would be perilous, but once inside, a person's presence in the glen would be impossible to detect. They would be the perfect place, I thought, to hide out, and I wondered if they had ever been used for that. Yet another place of refuge perhaps: a covert for Cairngorm fugitives maybe – Jacobites, Covenanters, outlaws, cattle-thieves and even wilderness-seeking aristocrats.

I stayed in the wood for a while, struck by how secluded it seemed. I had only been in Glen Feshie a day and a night, but I was already beginning to be affected by the place. Like all wild areas, it offered somewhere separate, somewhere detached from the conventions of everyday life. And perhaps that was the power of the place: that it could simultaneously conceal and recast our stories. It gave us the chance, even for the briefest of moments, to project an alternative narrative onto our lives, to hide or re-imagine our sense of identity.

The Duchess of Bedford must have felt the same thing. A connection through disconnection. By building the huts in Glen Feshie she had created a kind of alternative reality, a romantic construct, both literal and imaginative. A place to live out the Highland fantasies of Scott's novels, or, more quietly, to realise the same simple wonderment conveyed in her lover's paintings.

I stopped at the bothy on my return through the glen. Rain water dripped from the roof in fat, elliptical beads as I sheltered under the thin eaves of the gable end. I hungrily ate the remainder of my food, suddenly cold but not wanting to be inside. It was easy to understand why the huts had been built in this particular part of the glen. The entry that I had read in the bothy's visitor book seemed right. There was a certain tranquillity to the place. Not an obvious, definable feeling but the kind of vague serenity received almost with realising it.

As I left the bothy, I passed two pine trees. I had not noticed them on my inbound journey, but they were remarkable. Growing less than a foot apart, the lower limbs of each tree had developed inwardly towards the other, twisting and feeling their growth over time, through and around the other tree's branches until they had become locked in an embrace, each supporting the weight of the other.

The Lost Shelter

'So I will build my altar in the fields,
And the blue sky my fretted dome shall be,
And the sweet fragrance that the wild flower yields
Shall be the incense I will yield to Thee.'
        Samuel Taylor Coleridge, *To Nature*.

[Inscription on the Hutchison Memorial Hut, Coire Etchachan.]

By their very nature, mountains are often malevolent custodians; archivists of histories that are dark, as well as secret. The Cairngorm range is no exception. In the early 1970s, it was the location of the worst-ever tragedy in British mountaineering history. A disaster, not merely terrible in the scale of lives lost, but rendered more dreadful because of the ages of the victims and the circumstances in which they died.

On Saturday 20 November 1971, two parties of schoolchildren and their two instructors left the ski-centre car park in Coire Cas. The plan had been for both groups of children to explore the plateau; ascend the mountains of Cairn Gorm and Ben Macdui; and practise navigation skills and route-finding along the way. After walking across the tops they would descend to the relative safety of the Lairig Ghru, spend the night in the Corrour Bothy and leave the following day. As events unfolded, however, neither party would make it that far.

Deteriorating weather conditions hampered progress for both groups. Strengthening winds and heavy snowfall created blizzards that whipped ferociously across the plateau. By mid-afternoon on the Saturday it was clear that the route they had planned would be impossible to complete. The contingency for such an event was simple: to seek shelter in the Curran Bothy, one of several rudimentary, man-made refuges that existed on the plateau at that time.

In the nightmare scenario that ensued, only one group of children made it to the emergency shelter. Confused, tired and lost, the second and smaller group failed to locate the Curran. Instead they were forced to attempt a seemingly hopeless overnight bivouac in the exposed, snow-filled depression of the Feith Buidhe, the stream that would eventually give its name to the tragedy.

Unable to make it to the bothy and having spent two nights on the plateau, the group was eventually discovered on the morning of the third day. During that time five of the schoolchildren and a trainee instructor (herself only eighteen years old) had died. They were found only a short distance from the safety of the Curran Bothy.

The Curran, St Valery, Jean's Hut, Bob Scott's Bothy, the Sinclair Hut.

The names of the old Cairngorm shelters held an undeniable mystique for me. They seemed redolent of a bygone, pioneering era of mountaineering. A time, it seemed, when enthusiasm and exuberance appeared to outweigh adversity and a lack of proper equipment. Occasionally I had come across pictures of the shelters: grainy, black and white photographs, the buildings sometimes sheathed in snow, their outlines barely discernible in the landscape. In others there were the smiling faces of youthful climbers crowding a narrow entrance or lazing outside in summer: scruffy, unkempt, happy.

Most of the shelters have long since disappeared. Bob Scott's Bothy was destroyed by fire, rebuilt and destroyed by fire again; Jean's Hut and the Sinclair Hut became derelict or were dismantled; the Curran and the St Valery demolished. Elsewhere in the Cairngorms a few still remain: the tiny Garbh Coire Bothy that I had visited on my walk along the Dee; the Hutchison Memorial Hut in Coire Etchachan; the Fords of Avon Refuge and the famous Corrour Bothy.

There was one shelter, however, that had been largely forgotten about. It was neither actively used, nor completely yet vanished; instead, its continued existence had become something of a myth. For years, I had heard rumours about this mysterious refuge. That it was supposedly situated at over 3,000 feet somewhere on the steep western flank of Strath Nethy, but was almost impossible to find.

The positioning of the El Alamein refuge was a mistake. It was never intended to be built on the northern spur of the Cairn Gorm mountain, tucked literally out of sight and notionally out of mind in a rarely ventured-to part of the Cairngorms. The story goes that its placement was a navigational error. Built by members of 51st Highland Division and named after one their most famous battles, a mix-up in grid references led to its construction not on the high plateau, like its sister hut the St Valery, but on an incidental ridgeline. Distanced from major climbs and too close to the edge of the range to be of practical use, its obscurity and lack of purpose eventually became the reason for its survival.

Controversy had always surrounded the high-level

shelters, but the Feith Buidhe disaster further polarised opinion, dividing those in favour of the retention of the buildings and those calling for their removal. For many mountain-goers the shelters were an important part of the mountain experience: rough, makeshift accommodation used to extend time spent in the Cairngorms, or vital points of emergency refuge. Others, however, considered their mere presence on the plateau a risk: notoriously hard to locate, they created a false sense of security, inviting the inexperienced and unprepared to rely unrealistically on finding their protection – an often impossible task in winter.

Following recommendations of the Feith Buidhe Fatal Accident Inquiry a decision was made to remove all three of the Cairngorm high-level shelters. After several years of highly publicised and emotive debate, the Curran was eventually pulled down in June 1975. It was followed shortly afterwards by the St Valery, the tiny refuge above the climbs at Stag Rocks.

For whatever reason, the El Alamein never followed suit. Perhaps the momentum to remove all three of the huts slowed. More likely, the El Alamein's location meant it was deemed an irrelevance, a shelter hardly known about, let alone used. Instead, the hut discreetly avoided demolition and has passed through the decades since, quietly forgotten about but apparently still there: a jumble of rocks, clustered around a metal frame, barely noticeable among the broken moraine of the Strath Nethy hillside.

My plan was to try to locate the El Alamein refuge. By exploring the plateau, I also intended to reach the sites of the other two high-level shelters. In doing so, I would be making a kind of pilgrimage, retracing a generation of footsteps that had preceded mine.

I stood beneath a mechanised landscape. Above me, lines of ski-tows and chair-lifts trailed statically uphill, strung over ski-runs devoid of snow and people. The monorail of the Cairngorm funicular snaked its way towards the summit of Cairn Gorm, with vertebrae of metal bars, that from a distance looked vaguely animal in form. Across grassy slopes, picket fences bristled, dividing the hillside into hard angular segments. Higher up, I was able to make out the slow trudge of two workmen in fluorescent coats, and further above them, the flashing orange lights of their vehicle. Months earlier, in midwinter, Coire Cas would have been a hive of activity, one of the busiest ski areas in Britain. By the time I had arrived however, midweek in late May, the place felt deserted, dormant.

The corrie was an obvious choice of location for such a large conglomeration of ski infrastructure. It was north-facing and extended in a long concave bowl between two ridges that accommodated multiple runs of varying distance. It was also the most accessible of all the Northern Corries – the large glacial bite-marks that front the north-west aspect of the plateau in huge amphitheatres of rock, snow and ice.

From the ski car park, I took the south-west path that ran below two of the other Northern Corries. The wind was up, pushing clouds fast across the top of the plateau. I walked first below the entrance to Coire an t-Sneachda, the *Coire of the Snow*. The name was well deserved. From the path, the corrie still showed a winter scene. Snow lay at the base of the corrie and plastered the dark rock of its head wall. Ice ran like threads of a spider's web in between the patches, forming clusters branching and connecting, like dozens of neurons.

Intimate familiarity with these corries is recent. Like many of Scotland's wild recesses, the first recorded explorations of their vertical geographies only properly began with the advent of climbing. The earliest serious inspections of the Northern Corries occurred at the beginning of the twentieth century with a meeting of the Scottish Mountaineering Club in Aviemore in 1904. Harold Raeburn, the pioneering Edinburgh climber, is credited with making one of the first ascents when he climbed 'Pygmy Ridge', the neatly defined spine of rock leading up from one of the central gullies of Coire an t-Sneachda.

After these initial, tentative forays, however, the Northern Corries remained collectively uncharted for many years. The prospect of more reachable, dramatic routes in Glen Coe and Ben Nevis diverted the attentions of the relatively small band of gentleman climbers who were the primary exponents of climbing expansion at the time. The Great War then halted the progress of climbing in the Cairngorms and across Scotland for a generation. So much so, that by the early 1930s, many of Raeburn's routes had yet to be repeated or surpassed. It would take the seismic shifts in society caused by the First World War and the Great Depression to usher in a new breed of mountaineer: a climbing fraternity far removed from their middle-class predecessors, who would eventually shape new ideas of how the wild places of the Cairngorms and the rest of Britain were to be explored.

I followed the path as it curved and climbed, taking the western flank above the next of the Northern Corries, Coire an Lochain. From the ridge I looked across at the horseshoe bend of the corrie's cirque. It had all the appearance of being freshly gouged, as if only recently hewn from the mountain behind it. Clean columns of square-edged granite rose from a dark matrix of scree, gully and rock, breaking the skyline with sharp definition: black against the sky's blue.

A gap-tooth crack in the middle of the cliffs, known to climbers as Y-gully, funnelled down to the corrie's most obvious feature: a flat disc of pink-tinged granite, titled at an angle on the sharp incline of the corrie. From the ridge it was impossible to judge the exact size of the slab, but it was huge. In summer the Great Slab is visible from the Strathspey valley, and in winter the flat rock can be deadly. Accumulations of snow bond poorly with the smooth, slanting surface, sending regular avalanches into the corrie floor below.

One of the Cairngorm shelters, Jean's Hut, had once stood in Coire an Lochain. I knew of it of only distantly. Like most of the shelters, its history has not been preserved with any official meticulousness. Instead, like its own existence, the memory survives in fragmentary, personal recollections, as insubstantial and makeshift as the building itself.

It had first been built in Coire Cas as a memorial bequeathed by the father of a skier, Jean McIntyre Smith, killed on the slopes of the corrie. When the ski-centre opened in the early 1960s, the hut was moved to the entrance of Coire an Lochan. It became a well-used base for climbing the far corrie wall, until the mid-1980s, when, like the Curran, it became implicated in tragedy.

In January 1984, four young hillwalkers attempted to reach Jean's Hut during a winter storm. In the severe blizzard conditions, they were unable to locate the hut and instead tried to make their way out from the corries.

Despite their attempts to reach safety, they were overcome by exposure and three out of the four men were killed. Jean's Hut was subsequently dismantled, both its creation and removal instigated by terrible loss. From the slopes above the corrie, I was able to see where the hut would have been: accommodated on the underside of the plateau, close to two emerald-black lochans, which were recessed like eyes in the deep sockets of the corrie's hollow.

The Cairngorm shelters were exceptional. Not in their size, construction or age, but in their sheer abundance. No other mountain range in Britain can claim to have had such a proliferation of bothies and high-level refuges in such close proximity.

But to understand something of the shelters, their one-time profusion and their reasons for being, it is first necessary to understand something of the history of recreation and exploration in the Cairngorms.

The earliest recorded ascents of many of the Cairngorm mountains occurred at the beginning of the nineteenth century. The writer and historian, Ian Mitchell, credits many of the first written summit accounts to the redoubtable clergyman, the Rev. George Skene Keith. In the summer of 1810 Keith undertook a series of journeys into the heart of the Cairngorms. Ostensibly spurred by the scientific curiosity of the age, Keith first clambered up Lochnagar, barometer in hand, to measure the mountain's height.

Two days later, the minister and his companions ascended Beinn a' Bhuird and Ben Avon, and the following day completed an epic journey to the mountains of Braeriach and Cairn Toul, painstakingly recording measurements on the summits in torrential rain and wind.

Several months later, Keith returned yet again to the Braeriach plateau and in the same day ascended Ben Macdui and Cairn Gorm. It was a remarkable feat of stamina and tenacity considering the lack of accurate maps and the fact that he was two years shy of his sixtieth birthday.

Before Keith's scientific ventures, the Cairngorms had existed as a region outwardly unexplored. Like other mountainous areas of Scotland, the Cairngorms were perceived as being a hostile, vulgar environment. The prevailing opinion of the time was summed up in Daniel Defoe's description of the mountains of Lochaber in his 1727 publication *A Tour through the Whole Island of Great Britain* as 'a frightful country full of hideous desert mountains, and unpassable except to the Highlanders who possess the precipices'.

At the end of the eighteenth century, however, British attitudes to mountains began to change. The Enlightenment period had inspired scientific enquiry in the fields of geology and botany, prompting individuals to venture into hitherto unconsidered mountainous regions. Likewise the Picturesque and Romantic Movements inspired an aesthetic reconsideration of wild places. Mountains came to represent a pastoral ideal, a bucolic alternative to the overcrowded and industrialised urban centres, and the pre-eminent destination for seeing what the leading Victorian art critic and mountain aficionado, John Ruskin, claimed to be 'the beginning and the end of all natural scenery'.

Championed by artists and poets alike and increasingly accessible to a burgeoning professional class, the mountains and upland areas of Britain were gradually invested with an entirely new cultural identity and imaginative significance.

By the time John Hill Burton had written the first guide to the Cairngorms in 1864, the massif was no longer *terra incognita*. Queen Victoria had already summited a number of the major peaks; the landscape artist George Fennel Robson had painted several of the passes and hills; and the naturalist William MacGillivray had effectively charted the entire range in the course of his observational wanderings. What is more, deliberately visiting the mountains had become an activity in its own right. Considered a virtuous and invigorating experience, it appealed both to Victorian notions of personal endeavour and a new-found appreciation of natural beauty and the Sublime in landscape.

The Cairngorms soon became a tourist destination and John Hill Burton made a compelling case for their uniqueness. 'The depth and remoteness of the solitude, the huge mural precipices, the deep chasms between the rocks, the waterfalls of unknown height, the hoary remains of the primeval forest, the fields of eternal snow, and the deep black lakes at the foot of the precipices, are full of such associations of awe and grandeur and mystery, as no other scenery in Britain is capable of arousing.'

As the nascent sport of mountaineering took shape in the mid-nineteenth century, however, the Cairngorms and other British hills were initially overlooked. The pioneering group of amateur climbers who formed the Alpine Club in 1857 considered themselves primarily as 'Alpinists', concerned solely with the new and esoteric challenge of conquering the peaks of continental Europe. By the latter half of the century, though, attention turned to the possibility of exploring domestic ranges: in particular in Snowdonia, the Lake District and Scotland.

The first organised climbing explorations of Scotland's hills were originally aimed at preparing for Alpine ventures. Scotland's snow and ice was viewed purely as a convenient training ground for foreign expeditions. The formation, however, of the Scottish Mountaineering Club in 1889, acknowledged the value of Scotland's hills in their own right. W.W. Naismith, a Scottish member of the Alpine club and a founder of the Scottish Mountaineering Club recognised (with the chauvinistic overtones of the time) the unique challenges of 'snowcraft in Scotland', pointing out that in Scotland, compared to guided ascents in the Alps, 'the amateur must undertake all the reconnoitring, the fatiguing step-cutting, and the responsibility of anchoring the party in the event of a slip. Hence it is that climbing at home with rope and axe deserves to be ranked among the noblest forms of recreation. It is a grand school for prudence, self-reliance, endurance, and the other qualities that make up manliness; perhaps better training for a mountaineer than following even famous guides.'

For all the enthusiasm that the Scottish Mountaineering Club and the Cairngorm Club (formed a year earlier), generated for venturing in Scotland's hills, mountaineering in Scotland and the Cairngorms for many years remained the preserve largely of a small band of wealthy, middle-class individuals. For the vast majority of the Scottish population the thought of going into mountainous terrain for recreation would have been inconceivable. The long hours of the working week dictated the lives of the masses. Free time and the means of travelling to mountains were the exclusive privilege of an affluent few.

It was not until the start of the 1930s that access to the mountains of Scotland began to take the shape of a mass movement. Reductions in working hours, rises in the standard of living and improvements in the transport infrastructure enabled a small but growing portion of the Scottish population to reach previously unconsidered areas of domestic wilderness. Up until that point, 'fresh air', as the Glasgow writer and climber Alastair Borthwick observed, 'was still the property of moneyed men, a luxury open to the few'.

The demographics of Scottish climbing had by that time already begun to change irrevocably. The First World War, and in particular the large-scale losses to the officer class, had stunted a generation of the old guard of climbers, depleting the ranks of the established climbing clubs. Among those who did return, little enthusiasm remained to push the boundaries of climbing exploration.

Simultaneously, the advent of the Great Depression, sparked by the Wall Street Crash of 1929, created mass youth unemployment. In the industrial heartlands of Britain, large numbers of young people suddenly found themselves with nothing to occupy their days. For many, a coincidence of enforced leisure time and a desire to leave the drudgery of the city behind led to regular excursions into the mountains. For the very first time the working-classes were to partake *en masse* in the purposeful exploration of high and wild places.

Amid this tumultuous expansion of outdoor access a counter-culture began to emerge. Groups of city-dwellers, predominately young and working-class, formed small, informal outdoor clubs which were different in constituency and outlook to the established climbing clubs of old: loose affiliations of friends or workers intent on reaching the mountains by any means possible.

It was Borthwick who most succinctly captured the spirit of this popular climbing revolution. His book

The Lost Shelter

Always a Little Further remains perhaps the most evocative account of this or any other era in Scottish mountaineering. 'I went because there I found a world whose existence I had not been brought up to expect, and because I liked the people who lived in it,' Borthwick wrote. 'It was a young world, governed by the young . . . most of the people I met were my own age; people who, like myself, had only recently discovered that they could leave city, class, and the orthodoxy of their elders behind them at the week-ends.'

The 'weekenders' as they called themselves, were for the large part financially and logistically disadvantaged. Many would have to walk or hitchhike out of the city, tramping for hours before even reaching the mountains. Likewise accommodation, by necessity, needed to be cheap or completely free. The formation of the Scottish Youth Hostel Association in 1931 went some way towards providing an affordable form of lodgings in many of the main climbing areas. But for many, sleeping rough in bothies, barns, caves or howffs, became not just an obligatory pastime but a fundamental part of their outdoor journeying.

The wholesale democratisation of mountain exploration that had started in the 1930s was to have a lasting effect. The recreational use of shelters in isolated landscapes became commonplace. In the Cairngorms several remote and abandoned buildings were increasingly inhabited by mountaineers. Victorian bothies such as the Corrour, which had originally been built for deer-stalking, and Ryvoan, a former croft, were regularly filled by a growing number of climbers and hillwalkers, breaking long days in the range in the relative comfort afforded by a roof and a fire.

By the end of the Second World War the slopes and corries of the Cairngorms were bedecked with climbers, walkers and skiers. Military training acquired during the war had provided many servicemen with the skills and the enthusiasm to venture into the mountains long after the conflict had ended. The war had also driven improvements in clothing design and large surpluses of ex-military equipment became cheaply available for outdoor use. Similarly, the advent of formal outdoor education, the popularisation of skiing and improved road access meant the mountains of the Cairngorms had never been busier.

The existing shelters of the Cairngorms, few and far between, suffered from continual and unregulated use. Climbers in particular began to require the use of additional shelters: basic, purpose-built buildings with close access to the most remote of the Cairngorm climbs. By the 1950s, the first in a new wave of shelters were being built in the range, fixed points of orientation and harbourage that by the start of the 1970s would extend in a man-made constellation right across the Cairngorm wilderness.

The Curran Bothy had been situated at a natural junction on the plateau. It was built on the broad col between the mountains of Cairn Lochan in the north and Ben Macdui to the south. The col, like its derivation from the French word for neck, was an area of connection, a bridging point between the bulwark of the Northern Corries and the highest point in the range.

A confluence of winds met me at the col. The prevailing southerly I had trudged into was suddenly joined by stronger, less predictable gusts from the west, scooping upwards from the Lairig Ghru. It seemed a logical place to build a shelter: a refuge at a place of extreme exposure, a halfway point and crossroads in the wind. But the Curran Bothy was flawed, often left unusable by its positional shortcomings.

I recalled one particular photograph of the building, or more specifically a photograph of where the building should be. The photograph had been taken in winter. A group of hillwalkers sat resting and eating on the hard, snow-covered surface of the plateau. In the distance a cloudless blue sky banked against a white horizon. The image was unremarkable and unplaceable, a scene from practically anywhere high in the range, except for one small feature. In the middle of the group, protruding from the snow was a small orange tube. Viewed next to a photo of the Curran in summer months, the tube is immediately recognisable. The group in the photograph were sitting next to the ventilation pipe from the roof of the bothy. The building itself was encased somewhere beneath them within thousands of cubic metres of snow.

I stood near where the photo must have been taken, at the edge of Lochan Buidhe. The waters of the lochan rippled and bobbed in the wind, pitching upwards with small white crests. At the far edge of the lochan the land dipped away beyond sight, leaving a watery horizon with bright sky above. From here the water began a descent of thousands of feet, first towards the long, clear waters of Loch Avon, then onwards to join the Spey.

At the other side of the path the process was mirrored. An even smaller lochan drained westwards in the guise of the March Burn, disappearing into the hillside in a hydrographic vanishing act before reappearing in the Pools of

Dee. This was a place of finely balanced priorities: the watershed separating east and west, the shifting supremacies of wind and weather, and the subtle demarcations of the land.

A couple of kilometres to the south of the col was the oldest surviving shelter of the plateau: Sappers' Bothy. Burton describes coming across the strange scene of 'neither more nor less than a crowd of soldiers, occupying nearly the whole table-land of the summit . . . occupied in erecting a sort of dwelling for themselves – half tent, half hut'. Remarkably, the shelter Burton describes being built still partially exists. Now just a loose collection of stones, resembling a sheep pen more than a building, it had once housed the men from the Royal Engineers. The soldiers, known as 'Sappers', were part of the Ordnance Survey. In the summer of 1847 they mapped the area from their makeshift base near the summit of Ben Macdui, resting, living and working for several months from their mountain shelter.

Cloud bundled in as I left the col. The blue sky reduced to a distant corner. Hail followed shortly afterwards, carried on the strengthening wind, peppering my back like buckshot.

'The plateaux are often swept by gales and winds of hurricane force, especially in winter. The writer has often seen small gravel blowing in the wind and plants torn out by the roots, and the strongest man can be blown right over and thrown on the ground, or reduced to crawling on all fours.' Adam Watson's description of a Cairngorm storm, in the Scottish Mountaineering Club (SMC) district guide to the range, almost defied imagination.

'When a gale is accompanied by thick storms of ground drift, or worse, by heavy falling blizzards plus ground drift, or worse still by mist as well,' Watson explains, 'conditions can be extremely serious on the plateaux, making it suffocating and difficult to breathe, hard to open your eyes, impossible to see anything beyond your own feet, and unable to communicate with your party except one at a time by cupping an ear and shouting into it. In these respects the blizzards of the Cairngorms can be as bad as anywhere in the world.'

This was the type of account that had sent me scuttling from higher ground in the Cairngorms on many occasions, fearful of being caught in the blinding chaos that extreme weather conditions on the plateau can create. I had been lucky. I had never experienced anything near the true severity of a full winter storm in the Cairngorms. To endure such an event and survive would be to witness the most intense climatic conditions possible on these islands.

The Cairngorms are a place of statistical superlatives. Records are set here and rarely broken. The highest ever windspeed in the UK was captured by the automatic weather station on the summit of Cairn Gorm in January 1993 at 176mph; the lowest ever temperature in the UK, -27.2°C, was recorded in Braemar; and nowhere else in the country experiences more snowfall than the Cairngorms. The reasons are simple.

The Cairngorm plateau is the largest area of high ground in Britain. Huge numbers of square miles of the range lie at over 3,000 feet, making the area naturally prone to heavy snowfall, freezing temperatures and high winds. The relative inland position of the range also ensures something of a continental climatic effect compared with other significant mountainous areas in Britain, becoming warmer in summer and colder in winter than the seaboard ranges on Scotland's west coast, the Lake District and Snowdonia.

Extremes of weather can occur at any time of the year in the range. Snow can fall in any month and gales are common even in summer. I remembered reading one report in the *Cairngorm Club Journal* of a hillwalk in September 1959. Temperatures on this particular day in Aberdeen were some of the warmest of the year. Yet high on the plateau the wind was of a 'terrible strength', combining with low cloud and driving rain to create conditions unthinkable fifty kilometres further east.

One of my favourite, most thrilling accounts of Cairngorm weather, however, comes from another iconic work of Scottish mountaineering literature. *Mountaineering in Scotland* by W. H. Murray recounts the exploits of the climbing elite of the 1930s and is a literary counterpoint to Alastair Borthwick's cult classic; a celebrated foil to the lesser-known mountaineering tales of the common man in Borthwick's *Always a Little Further*. Yet both works of literature share an obvious similarity: a determined fervour for exploring Scotland's mountains that somehow overcame the technical limitations of equipment available at the time. To the modern reader, blessed with mobile communications, satellite navigation systems and high-specification clothing, the books are at times both horrifying and humbling.

Murray's description of his Cairngorm blizzard recounts a terrifying ordeal. An experienced mountaineer, Murray grasps the severity of the impending storm, as he watches 'a great change overtaking the sky'. From his position high on the plateau he is able to witness 'in every direction, as far as the eye could see . . . an unbroken mass of dark storm-clouds, rapidly pressing down upon the mountain like a leaden canopy.'

Murray and his companion have no choice but to continue onwards from the remote interior of the range, as 'it became obvious that a snow-storm must at any moment close down on us. The flakes came faster and faster, at first fat and whirling, then driving and vicious, applying an icy lash to the cheek'. The pair are soon consumed by the storm that comes down 'like the wrath of God', their woollen balaclavas becoming 'a mass of icicles', their breeches 'stiff as a board' and their chests 'encased in breastplates of white armour'.

In conditions typical of the worst kinds of Cairngorm storm, the two men experience an episode of almost complete sensory deprivation. 'The visibility had fallen to almost nil, and for twenty minutes thereafter we could not see beyond our boots. Below, above, on all sides, was the impalpable writhing whiteness, which left the eye nothing to focus on, nothing to which one could relate one's own body . . . We had the sensation of floating rather than walking.' Added to this is the noise, 'the pulsing blast of the storm' and the 'fierce instant *swish* of loose powder sweeping across the snow-fields'.

Murray and his climbing partner battled through the conditions, labouring through drifting snow and against the wind, probing for the ever-present danger of cornices, all the while navigating through impossibly featureless terrain. They eventually descended from the plateau before nightfall, badly affected by their experiences. Murray's partner had frostbitten hands and Murray himself verged dangerously towards hypothermia. 'Rarely have I been more exhausted and numbed with cold, which now gripped not only the extremities but the whole body.'

The men walked a further fifteen kilometres before completing their epic journey. But back within the relatively temperate surroundings of their destination they experienced what amounts to a strange readjustment in reality. They found themselves questioning the recollections of their recent struggle and doubting that such testing conditions could have ever really existed. 'Already the wild turmoil far above our heads seemed infinitely remote; and the Braeriach plateau, like some lost continent of the skies.'

—

The hail thinned to sleet as I followed the sunken course of the Feith Buidhe burn eastwards. Eventually the land gave way and the waters toppled down the slick, black cliffs next to the long vertical slope of Hell's Lum Crag. From here my best chance of finding where the St Valery hut had been located would be to track the edge of the plateau, walking the rim of the deep Loch Avon basin until I reached the promontory of flat ground above Stag Rocks.

During the brief years of its existence the St Valery hut had been notoriously hard to find. Positioned above the exit point for several major climbing routes, the St Valery straddled a wide featureless expanse on one side and a terrifying void on the other. In the appalling weather conditions during the Feith Buidhe disaster, even an experienced mountain rescue team, tasked with checking the hut, failed to locate it; instead, they became embroiled in their own personal battle of survival on the plateau that night.

For a kilometre, I walked with an eagle eye's view of the landscape, scanning the valley far below. From high above, the land appeared in virtual relief, the real-life version of my map's exactitudes, equivalent but packed with colour and detail: the thin crescent of golden sand curving around the western end of Loch Avon, the turquoise waters and the jumbles of dark glacial moraine, deceptively miniaturised by my high viewpoint.

I reached the flat slabs of granite that shelved out above Stag Rocks and began to look around, not entirely sure of what I was searching for. Perhaps the site of the St Valery would be obvious, a perfect section of level ground, the intuitive spot on which to build the shelter. I clambered round the rocky outcrops but found nothing, no clear sign of where the hut had once been.

The St Valery had been built primarily as a climbers' refuge. Unlike the Curran, it was significantly distanced from the most direct walking or ski-touring traverses heading to or from the Northern Corries. Instead, it was the most vital of shelters, a place of rest and relative safety after the completion of some the best winter routes in the Cairngorms. Climbs such as 'The Chancer', 'Hell's Lum' and 'Afterthought Arete' all finished within easy walking distance of where the hut had been.

The hut when it was constructed in 1962 had not been the first of its kind. A decade earlier, members of the Kincorth Mountaineering Club from Aberdeen built the first in a series of rough shelters or 'howffs' in the isolated Glen Slugain. Intended as way-stations on the long walk to the crags of Beinn a' Bhuird, the howffs were built into several of the natural shelter-points of the glen. Inconspicuous and barely visible except to those who knew of their existence, the howffs became the retreat of a select band of climbers – secret shelters. One of these shelters still remains in use today and is described in nostalgic detail in Dave Brown and Ian Mitchell's book, *Mountain Days and Bothy Nights*. Miraculously its location is still largely unknown, guarded by the 'word-of-mouth free-masonry which maintains its seclusion'.

Several more, much less discreet, shelters soon sprang up across the Cairngorms. In 1954, the Hutchison Memorial Hut was built in a large area of open ground near Loch Etchachan. A small but sturdy hut, the Hutchison is still easily visible today behind the northern slopes of Derry Cairngorm. Three years later Edinburgh University Officer Cadets built the Sinclair Hut. Placed at the northern end of the Lairig Ghru, the Sinclair Hut was intended to complement the more southerly Corrour Bothy, but looked desperately at odds with its surroundings. A blocky, utilitarian stone building, with one small window and a corrugated iron roof, the Sinclair Hut was eventually demolished in 1991.

Further shelters were to follow. The 1960s witnessed the largest number of refuges built across the massif. Within the space of only a few years the St Valery and the El Alamein, the Garbh Coire Bothy, the Fords of Avon Bothy and the Curran all came into existence. Had it not been for the tragic events of November 1971, perhaps even more shelters would have been constructed, expanding the network of refuges to other remote corners of the range and beyond.

Instead, the Feith Buidhe disaster happened, and with it, the inevitable facing up to many difficult questions. Choices about how wild places like the Cairngorms are to be understood; of how our relationship with the mountains is to be defined; and ultimately of how we interact with an environment so potentially at odds with the requirements of human survival.

As I turned to leave, I caught sight of something perched on one of the south-facing slabs. A rectangular stone tablet, grey against the pink rock. I moved towards it to get a closer look. It was a plaque, roughly two feet by one foot, with florid dots of lime-green lichen pock-marking the surface like cultures growing in a petri dish.

Running across the centre, barely noticeable at first, was an incised line of text. The letters had worn back into rock like the weathered writing on a gravestone. I angled my head to see the indented shadows of each letter and read the words out loud: St Valery Refuge. Below, there was a date: 1962, the numbers now hardly visible, melting into stone. Above the writing there was a symbol: HD in capital letters set within a circle, the insignia of Highland Division – the men who built St Valery.

I had not expected to find anything of the St Valery still remaining. I presumed the refuge had been demolished with all the impassioned zeal that had once characterised the debate about the high-level shelters, and with it, the removal of all evidence of its existence. Yet here was the most iconic relic of the refuge left behind. A consciously placed memento to those who had once used it. It seemed to me an undeniably poignant gesture.

My unexpected discovery at Stag Rocks spurred me northwards, across the rolling levels of the plateau, over soft grasses and clumps of purple mountain azaleas, back towards my starting point and the ridgeline that held the remains of the lost shelter of El Alamein.

Wilderness ended as I reached the summit of Cairn Gorm. People huddled in groups, rifling through their rucksacks, eating and leaning close to talk through the wind. Above them the industrial metal tower of the weather station dominated the skyline. I stepped into the wind-shadow of the building and hunkered down next to its thick, stainless-steel door. In the stone wall opposite me was a profusion of brightly coloured food wrappers, stuffed in between the gaps in the rocks like lurid flowers.

I left the summit in a procession of people. A human ant-trail moving up and down the litter-strewn path from the huge spaceship-shaped Ptarmigan restaurant at the top of the funicular railway. After a few minutes I broke free of the mass march, crossing eastwards under a ski-tow and re-entering more desolate terrain.

I had a grid reference for the El Alamein hut. It was marked on my map with a small red dot, just below an obvious spur of flat ground to the north of the peak Cnap Coire na Spreaidhe. The weather had begun to clear; the strong winds had blown through the day's earlier squalls and blue sky had returned in large, broken sections. The shelter, I thought, would be easy to find.

For almost two hours I paced the ridgeline from Cnap Coire na Spreidhe, moving back and forth from one pile of rocks to another, convinced that each granite formation was the stone-clad shelter I was looking for. I cursed myself for not bringing binoculars.

The small red dot I had marked seemed increasingly elusive. I checked and rechecked my position against the map, but after a while I began to doubt my navigation. There appeared to be little scope for error. In one direction, the land slipped steeply down into Strath Nethy's deep ravine just as the contour lines suggested, and in the other ran the finger of ridgeline that extended from the summit of Cairn Gorm. The shelter was surely some-where in between.

I settled down amongst some boulders to consider the alternative possibilities. Either the grid reference I had come across for the El Alamein was unreliable, or I was just too late. Perhaps the shelter had simply crumbled back into the mountain. Perhaps I was, at that moment, sitting amongst the clutter of its remains. Perhaps its myth had been spawned from its very dissolution. Perhaps the shelter was now truly lost.

For months afterwards, I harboured a nagging uncer-tainty about the demise of the El Alamein. It was an outlying thought, hidden away like the shelter itself, that I returned to again and again. I wanted to believe that the El Alamein still existed somewhere and that I had sim-ply been unable to find it. So in late autumn, only weeks before the first snowfalls of the winter arrived, I returned to the Northern Corries to search for the shelter once again.

My plan was to be methodical, to contour back and forth pedantically at different levels of the ridge, retracing the steps of my last visit and enlarging my area of search. In the end though, I didn't need to.

I found the shelter almost immediately, barely twenty feet below where I had walked earlier in the year. I wondered how I could have so comprehensively missed it last time. I felt inwardly embarrassed at my naviga-tional ineptitude, but consoled myself with the thought that perhaps an optical illusion had been at play. From above and in dull light, the upright wall of rocks profiling flatly against the stony terrain must have had an almost uniform surface appearance, seeming one-dimensional next to the slope. Now, though, in intense sunlight and shadow, the shelter appeared in clear definition. It was a prism-shaped pile of rocks on a small shelf of flat ground that edged out above the deep descent into Strath Nethy.

The El Alamein was like nothing I had ever seen before on a Scottish hillside and I was astounded at the sight of it. Its position seemed improbable. Teetering on what looked to be the last available patch of horizontal land before an almost sheer drop into the glen below, it reminded me of mountain structures I had seen in the Alps: hay-barns and cattle-sheds perched on tiny balconies of grass thousands of feet above deep glacial valleys.

Perhaps it had been the disappointment of not finding the shelter the first time, or the months of ruminating about its possible whereabouts, or simply the uniqueness of its form and position, but the refuge seemed no less enigmatic, no less exceptional in real life. More so in fact.

The construction looked worryingly unstable. Rocks of various sizes had been stacked with an unfathomable logic of placement, forming both the outer walls and the roof of the building. In between the boulders, a natural mortar had developed. Vivid green mosses and grasses grew where, over time, earth had collected in the gaps. At the base of the wall nearest to me, I found another granite tablet, similar to the one at Stag Rocks, placed like a keystone with rocks loaded upon it. This time the engraved writing was much clearer: 'El Alamein Refuge', and '1963', had been carved expertly in an elegant serif font.

At the narrow entranceway there was a small metal door. I pushed it gently and it creaked open on its metal frame. The internal framework was wrought iron, rusted to a deep umber. Vertical shafts had been cemented into ground with the roof supports bolted to them at forty-five degree angles. A metal mesh had been welded to the structure and sack cloth hung around it. Running the length of the shelter, a leftover section of the mesh had been bent double and was fixed as a six-foot long bench.

It felt calm inside, protected and enclosed, despite a quarter of the roof missing. It reminded me somehow of a grotto, a deliberately conceived place of reflection and veneration. No longer a place of practical purpose, but a curiosity, a mountain artefact. A structure not just to be linked to one terrible event, but representative of an entire mountaineering cultural heritage – the embodiment of centuries of exploration of Scotland's high places and a reminder of a time when seeking shelter in the Cairngorms was not only a necessity but an integral part of the outdoor experience.

Final Flight

'I know that I shall meet my fate
Somewhere among the clouds above.'
W. B. Yeats, *An Irish Airman Foresees His Death*.

A small plane tracked a course northwards through the night sky, breaking the silence of the empty glen. I followed its progress from my sleeping bag far below, watching its navigation lights blink against the darkness. Eventually, the drone of engine noise faded as the aircraft slipped from view, disappearing behind one of the most remote areas of high ground, not only in the Cairngorm range, but in the whole of mainland Britain.

Beinn a' Bhuird is a peak whose isolation can only properly be quantified when viewed against the blank areas it occupies on a map. Such is the mountain's geographical separation from established, man-made features that, cartographically, if you were to draw a circumference from its summit to the nearest public road, the smallest possible radius would be at least ten kilometres.

I had covered most of this distance on mountain bike, riding by the light of my head-torch along the dusty forest track of Glen Quoich. More than once I had almost fallen off, my front wheel lurching into deep, dry ruts or hitting unseen rocks on the path. My large rucksack didn't help either, raising my centre of gravity and listing me sideways with even the slightest of movements. At one point, I even thought about walking as a safer option, but in the darkness, the kilometres ahead seemed too monotonous to contemplate on foot.

It was, however, the remoteness of Beinn a' Bhuird that had drawn me there and the story of an event unintentionally but fundamentally connected with the isolation of this part of the plateau. An incident that, like many others at the time, initiated a collective responsibility for recovery and rescue in Britain's mountains.

＿＿

On 14 January 1945, in the concluding months of World War Two, an Oxford MkI aeroplane of 311 Squadron took off from RAF Tain in Aberdeenshire. The flight should have been uneventful and routine: a non-combat mission to an RAF base at Hornchurch in the south of England. Weather conditions at the time of departure were recorded as favourable – clear skies and low winds – and the crew consisted of five highly experienced airmen from the Free Czechoslovak Air Force. Yet the small training aircraft failed to reach its intended destination.

For many months afterwards its whereabouts remained a mystery. There were no records of the plane landing at an alternative airfield and there had been no reports of a crash-site. The aircraft and its crew, it seemed, had simply disappeared. It was not until eight months later that the fate of the Oxford eventually became known. Two hill-walkers discovered the plane's wreckage and the remains of the five crew members, high on the summit plateau of Beinn a' Bhuird. The nature of this rarely ventured to part of the Cairngorms had rendered the immediate discovery of the downed plane practically impossible. But the Oxford's crash-site was no means unique. By the end of the Second World War, the existence of aircraft wreckage in such high and remote settings throughout Britain had become tragically commonplace.

I had once before come across the debris of an aircraft in the hills. I had been walking on an unmarked route in an empty corner of the Ochils – the prominent band of volcanic ground that rises sharply from the flood plains of the River Forth.

The terrain was difficult and slow-going: hundreds of soft peat-hags formed small grassy islands across the moorland summit. I constantly had to jump over the channels of dark bog that ran in between. During one leap something caught my eye. A loose collection of metal shapes, part-buried but protruding from the black soil. The metal had rusted and looked twisted and malformed. It was impossible to guess its original use, but curious as to their origin, I searched around for other pieces.

On harder ground, near a fence line, I found a larger pile of fragments, heaped together in a small mound – metal of varying shapes and sizes, machine components, once part of something larger, now jumbled out of context and gradually dissolving into the hillside. I knew it must have been from a plane, for nothing else could have been brought to such a high and unreachable place.

During the Second World War literally hundreds of planes crashed on the high ground of Britain. In 1943 alone, military crashes had accounted for the deaths of 571 aircrew on the mountains of Britain. The numbers of crashes reduced dramatically in the years immediately after the war but still remained a relatively common occurrence. Part of the reason lay in the absence of knowledge about the unique atmospheric conditions that are created among Britain's mountainous areas.

The ice-age formations of Scotland's mountains, in particular, have significant implications for aircraft. The deep corries and glens that are so typical of glaciation are now known to be responsible for meteorological phenomena that can severely disrupt airflow in and around higher ground.

The effects of these conditions can be considerable. 'Rotor streaming', for instance, can occur when air moves swiftly over mountains, creating revolving eddies of wind-current moving the air in sudden down-draughts and uplifts in, or around the summit level. 'Standing waves' also develop on the lee side of mountains, forming oscillating patterns of air flow that can cause extreme forms of turbulence.

It is unknown if such atmospheric conditions on the Beinn a' Bhuird massif were responsible for the crash of the Oxford. Yet remarkably, barely three years earlier, another flight had crashed only a few kilometres away on the mountain's south-facing ridge: a Wellington Mk Ia on a night navigation exercise from RAF Lossiemouth had flown into Beinn a' Bhuird's snow covered slopes, apparently mistaking them for low cloud. Tragically, but astonishingly, only two out of the seven airmen on board the Wellington died in the crash.

These accidents were not isolated incidents in the Cairngorms. Over the years the range has held a deadly siren call for aircraft. The upper reaches of Braeriach still harbour the remains of two wartime crashes, whilst the summit of Ben Macdui witnessed the crash of another training aeroplane on a non-combat mission in 1942, and more recently the mid-air collision of two United States F15 fighter-jets in 2001.

Nan Shepherd knew something about the lethal magnetism that the Cairngorms could exert. She had her own theories as to why the plateau was so perilous to aviators.

During the Second World War more planes (mostly training planes) crashed here than one cares to remember. Like the unwary of older days who were drowned while fording swollen streams, or dashed from the precipices they attempted to climb, these new travellers underestimated the mountain's power. Its long flat plateau top has a deceptive air of lowness; and its mists shut down too swiftly, its tops are too often swathed in cloud, pelting rain or driving snow . . . for liberties to be taken with its cruel rock.

The sheer number of plane wrecks in the Cairngorms and across Britain's mountains is telling, not merely as a matter of historical record, but also as a contemporary moral statement. That so many should exist, yet so little be known of their existence seems lamentable, even shameful. I struggled in vain to find any meaningful information on the Cairngorm air crashes. What details had been collected appeared to have been gathered by enthusiasts: a small band of unconnected individuals who had taken it upon on themselves to visit crash sites and record their findings.

The pastime appeared, at first, ghoulish, driven in equal measure by morbid curiosity and obsessiveness. I came across photos of individuals standing slightly abashed and setting scale among wreckage, out of print books with lists of grid references in obscure locations and websites meticulously updated with new findings.

The more I researched the Cairngorm air crashes, however, the more I came to respect these aviation historians. It became clear that, for most, there was a deeper sense of purpose to their pursuits. Their intention was not to plunder or trophy-hunt, but to chronicle and inform. To ensure that long after the wreckage had sintered into the mountains, a memory would be preserved, and that those who died would be not be forgotten. I also felt a similarity in our explorations. Their ventures to remote hillsides, often alone and in terrible weather, in search of uncertain fragments of history, seemed to echo the journeys I was making in the Cairngorms.

I was keen to find out more about the Oxford's final flight, its circumstances and its consequences. The crash-site and whatever wreckage remained were too significant, too important to ignore. These were secret histories for sure. But secret histories that deserved not to be so.

At dawn, Beinn a' Bhuird was enshrouded in mist. The cloud level had descended during the night and held a fixed line like an atmospheric spirit level, contouring evenly around the hillside and dividing the mountain in two: above and below, seen and unseen. To enter into such dense, delineating cloud would be like stepping behind a curtain. The visible world would be left behind within the space of a dozen footsteps.

I struggled to summon up enthusiasm to begin the climb. Instead, I lingered at a lower level, exploring the woodland that curved around the mountain's southern flanks.

The trees here were ancient and undisturbed, the perfect habitat for wildlife rarely seen anywhere else in the country. I had heard from a friend that this large stand of Scots pines was the territory of a creature as elusive as it could be terrifying, an animal as likely to flee in shy retreat as it was prone to close quarters suddenly in unprovoked attack.

Capercaillie are one of Britain's biggest ground birds, a huge woodland grouse, roughly the size of a turkey. The male bird is spectacular and unmistakable, with its blue-black plumage, shimmering, petrol-green chest feathers and rufous wings. It also possesses a call as distinctive as its appearance: a series of bizarre clicking and popping noises bearing an uncanny resemblance to a cork being pulled from a wine bottle. Yet despite its size and uniqueness, it is a bird seldom encountered; a species now characterised in part by its rarity.

Populations of the capercaillie in Britain are in serious decline. The total number of birds has been falling dramatically since the 1970s. The reasons are multiple and diverse. Changes in weather patterns in recent years have affected breeding, with wetter, colder summers increasing chick mortality. Predation, most notably from other birds and foxes, as well as a rise in deaths from collisions with deer-fencing, has also contributed to a decrease in capercaillie numbers. Most important, though, has been the gradual decline of their preferred habitat: the mature, coniferous remnants of the Caledonian Forest.

That morning, at first light, I stalked the ancient rides and clearings of the Glen Quoich woodland. For an hour I trod softly through heather and blaeberry, feeling the plants rebound gently under my feet. At the edges of tree trunks I came across wedges of bright orange fungus, the colour of pine resin. I saw spider webs, dew-covered and strung from the right-angled limbs of trees. Where branches had fallen to the ground they had become barnacled with a covering of delicate, mint-green lichen.

The place seemed perfect for Capercaillie: the trees were large and well spaced, ideal for roosting and accommodating the bird's ungainly flight paths. There was an extensive understorey too, essential for breeding and for cover.

I had read not only about the reclusiveness of caper-caillies, but also about their aggression. 'Rogue' males had been known to assault passing cars and unsuspecting humans. One book even recorded an incident of cyclist being dislodged from his bike in a capercaillie attack. I felt excited and apprehensive at the prospect of seeing one. The forestry, though, was silent, and I was soon above the tree-line ascending a path on the westernmost shoulder of Beinn a' Bhuird. A few hundred metres above me, the cloudbase loomed ominously. It was being blown fast across the hillside, but was constantly replenished on a strengthening wind, an opaque band of colourless, viscous mist.

—

I was procrastinating. Stalling my entry into the clouds for a long as possible as I sat and ate chocolate and planned my route. The wreckage of the Oxford lay roughly two kilometres northeast from the summit, across a wide expanse of featureless terrain. In clear weather, the passage presented little difficulty: a short walk across the high tableland with views stretching out in every direction. In low visibility, however, the plateau here would become a bewildering area of obscurity and sameness, unreadable and disorientating.

By taking a series of bearings from the summit cairn I hoped to locate Stob an t-Sluichd, the thin spur of land slipping away to the north. It was here, near a set of rocky outcrops, that the plane's debris was scattered. Significant fragments apparently still remained there, including the two huge engines of the aircraft.

As I studied the map I suddenly realised exactly where I was. I had stopped to rest on the slopes above a deep-lying stream, the Alltan na Beinne. I recognised the name immediately. It was here, on the angled descent towards the V-shaped cleft of the burn, that one of Britain's most incredible stories of mountain survival once took place.

In the final weeks of December 1964, the Cairngorms were subject to several periods of prolonged and heavy snow, punctuated by both a hard frost and three days of slight thaw. The climatic factors were to prove influential in the events that later occurred, when four young men, Alexander Mackenzie, Alasdair Murray, Robert Burnett and Alexander McLeod, embarked on their winter ascent of Beinn a' Bhuird. The friends, all of whom were involved in the Scouting movement, were experienced hillwalkers. They had planned to make their expedition to Beinn a' Bhuird over two days. The would walk in from Luibeg Bothy near Derry Lodge, reaching the summit by the same gradual south-western route that I was taking, before descending to spend the night among the pine trees of Glen Quoich. By the time the walkers had reached the summit plateau of Beinn a' Bhuird, however, conditions had become serious. Driving snow, low visibility and a strong north-westerly wind forced the friends to leave the mountain's south top using the gully of a small stream, the Allt Tarsuinn, to guide them.

The men descended on the north side of the burn, with Alasdair Murray leading the way. Beneath their feet lay a substantial accumulation of snow. The north-westerly winds that had blown transversely across the slope had deposited a hard wind-slab that felt deceptively solid underfoot.

During the descent Murray slipped and fell some distance into the gully. Unhurt by the fall he began climbing back up towards his friends. Instead, Robert Burnett shouted down to him to cross to the opposite bank and continue down on the windward side of the stream, which by comparison was curiously devoid of snow. The men would then regroup at the bottom. The instruction from Burnett was undoubtedly to save Murray's life.

Within minutes of Murray's fall, the snow on the north side of the burn had fractured, breaking apart in a massive slab avalanche that consumed his three companions. Immediately afterwards, Murray searched the avalanche debris, frantically probing the huge area of white moraine for signs of life. His efforts, though, proved futile. After half an hour of searching, Murray ran for help, crossing more than eight kilometres of hard terrain to reach the nearest point of human contact – Mar Lodge.

A rescue party was raised, but time was of the essence. The lives of the three men buried in the snow depended on their rapid location and extraction. The search team managed to cover the long distance to Beinn a' Bhuird by vehicle, but their efforts at first seemed in vain. In the early hours of the following morning, searching by fading torchlight in the cold winter night, a tragic discovery was made. The body of one of the group, Alexander McLeod, was pulled from the snow.

At that point, hope of finding the remaining two men alive must have all but vanished. But at daybreak, with the rescue party reinforced by soldiers from Aberdeen, the search continued. Several more hours passed without success, until at midday, one of the rescuers noticed a small hole in the avalanche debris. Unusually, the opening was yellowed at its edges. As the rescuer peered inside, he heard a voice. It came from Robert Burnett. He was trapped, but alive. Incredibly, he had managed to survive for over twenty-two hours entombed within the snow, the longest period of survival from a Scottish avalanche burial on record and one of the longest known survivals in complete contact with snow anywhere in the world.

Burnett's escape was remarkable and fortuitous, owing much to the perseverance of the makeshift rescue team as well as the luck of his eventual positioning within the avalanche debris. Burnett had been buried lying on his back within the snow. With amazing good fortune, both of his hands had become lodged above his head and he was able to bore a small cavity above his face. In doing so, he had, by chance, exposed an air passage that funnelled through the blocky debris to the surface of the snow. Alexander Mackenzie, the final member of the group to be accounted for, unfortunately was not so lucky. His body was discovered shortly afterwards.

Despite Burnett's miraculous survival, the Beinn a' Bhuird avalanche was sadly an otherwise unsurprising event. It conforms closely to our modern understanding of avalanche anatomy and causation. For a start there had been a considerable build-up of snow in the preceding weeks, providing the necessary quantities for a significant and dangerous accumulation in the snowpack.

Unlike Alpine regions where large avalanches predominately occur within 24 hours of the initial snowfall, the avalanche risk in Scotland can extend for longer periods in cold weather. Wind can redistribute snow with dramatic effect, simplifying its crystalline structure so that it bonds in a tighter, more cohesive form. Areas of redistributed snow will then collect in dense slabs in leeward positions on top of existing levels of snowfall. Often, the resulting wind-slab will appear deceptively firm and well-compacted, prompting, as it did for the four men on Beinn á Bhuird, an entirely false sense of safety.

The danger, however, arises from stratification, the layering effect that results from successive accruals of differing ages and deposits of snow. When the bonds between the varying layers become too weak, an avalanche will occur. This was almost certainly the reason for the Beinn a' Bhuird incident. The massive slab that sheared from the gully's slopes was undoubtedly newer snow detaching from old, released along an historic fault-line in the snowpack, most probably created during the thawing or frost that had occurred in the weeks before the avalanche.

It is clear that the four hillwalkers were not fully aware of the potential perils they faced on Beinn a' Bhuird. Avalanche information at the time was rudimentary compared to present-day knowledge. Burnett later described the avalanche as being a 'chance in a million', a misconception of rarity later to be used by Bob Barton and Blyth Wright as the title of their seminal book on Scottish avalanches. But even today, avalanche assessment remains an inexact science. At best, it is an educated guess. A measure of likelihood coarsely calibrated on a scale of one to five – probability theory pitched against the fickle contingencies of snow.

—

Policemen, estate-workers, climbers and gamekeepers, the impromptu rescue team gathered for the Beinn a' Bhuird avalanche was an eclectic mix of individuals. They were local volunteers from different walks of life who were willing and able to respond to the call for help. It was a typically informal and largely untrained assemblage that was not only commonplace for search and rescue missions at the time, but quite often the sole lifeline for those lost or injured in the hills. It was in truth, a tradition of established but unacknowledged heroism, a recurring act of altruism that had quietly existed in the Cairngorms and other mountainous areas of Britain for decades.

One of the first recorded incidents of such volunteer-led rescue efforts in Britain's mountains was the search for the Reverend Henry Wellington Starr. In September 1846, Starr travelled to north Wales on the advice of his doctor. Like the spa towns of England, the mountains of Snowdonia were, at the time, fast gaining a reputation for their curative, health-giving properties and Starr was keen to experience their benefits. Neither an experienced hill-man nor local to the area, he was unfamiliar with the terrain and the conditions. After venturing alone onto the mist-covered slopes of Snowdon, Starr must have encountered an environment far beyond his understanding or abilities and he promptly disappeared.

A search party of colossal proportions was raised. For three days, 900 people were reported to have scoured the slopes and valleys of the massif. The enormous number of rescuers was unprecedented, but perhaps not entirely compelled by a collective moral duty. A large reward had been posted for Starr's safe return and undoubtedly the reputation of the area's burgeoning trade in therapeutic tourism was also at stake. Despite the huge volume of volunteers, the extraordinary rescue attempt was unsuccessful. The body of the errant curate was not found until the following year, in Cwm Brwynod at the foot of a large precipice.

As the new pastime of climbing on Britain's hills and crags gained a growing popularity in Victorian society, so too did the number of accidents happening in upland areas. Searches of the Welsh mountains and Lake District in particular, were to occur with increasing frequency. In *A Perilous Playground* – the most definitive book about regional mountain rescues in Britain – Bob Maslen-Jones recounts the mounting number of rescue attempts that took place in Snowdonia from the mid-nineteenth century onwards.

On one occasion, on 30 August 1894, the third attempt to climb 'Slanting Gully' on the north face of Lliwedd resulted not only in tragedy but also in the involvement of a group of local miners, and serves as an early illustration of the risks taken and the commitment of individuals involved in mountain rescue.

John Mitchell, a climber from Oxford, had ascended a considerable height of Slanting Gully unassisted, before he slipped from a ledge near the top of the climb. Much to the horror of his companions watching from below, Mitchell fell over 40 metres into the gully floor. Unable to climb the necessary distance to reach the stricken climber, but almost certain of the fatal outcome of the fall, Mitchell's companions summoned help from nearby.

Men from the local copper mine volunteered to retrieve Mitchell's body. Maslen-Jones's account of the incident is noteworthy, in particular, for one specific section that includes a quote by the original narrator of the events. The short description hints at a sense of dedication and competence, as well as compassion: the age-old attributes of modern mountain rescue. 'The way in which these men accomplished their task is worthy of the highest praise, one of them descending the whole way alongside the body and preventing further injury, whilst the last man had to come down without any aid whatsoever.'

The regularity of mountaineering accidents soon caused more widespread concern amongst the climbing community. A turning point came in 1903 when four climbers were fatally injured in a fall on Scafell Crags in the Lake District. The 'Scafell Disaster' proved to be a pivotal moment in the history of British mountain rescue. Within a year of the disaster, a shared sense of fraternal anguish among mountaineers proved a catalyst for action. The dearth of available rescue equipment prompted the installation of mountain rescue posts in key areas. In reality, these were little more than caches of rudimentary medical supplies, but nonetheless they set a precedent as the first attempt to create a collective accountability for rescue in Britain's mountains.

The rescue posts were duly maintained, replenished and added to. But there was little appetite for further wholesale development. It would take yet another climbing accident, over twenty-five years later, to set in motion the true beginnings of a national organisation for mountain rescue.

Entering into the clouds felt like crossing a threshold, moving from one dimension into another: from the solid into the vaporous. Within seconds the horizon had disappeared; detail and landscape were dulled and then lost. Visibility had been reduced to a few dozen metres and I began to angle each footfall in line with the small red indicator arrow on my compass. The wind had risen too: a steady barrage of gusts blowing in from the south-east.

Time, like distance, became hard to judge. Minutes passed by slowly as the ground beneath me repeated itself on the long upward slog. I became locked into a strange perambulatory trance, a feeling of stationary movement on a treadmill of tussocks and boulders.

The incline eventually gave way and the wind gelled the air into a thick, oppressive force. I had reached the plateau and felt a growing sense of disorientation. Uphill was at least a direction; now flatness added to my navigational uncertainty. I remembered the summary of Beinn a' Bhuird that I had read in the SMC Munro guide. It had described the area in commanding terms: as a 'vast mountain' that has 'one of the biggest tablelands in the Cairngorms'. As I tracked the edge of the mountain's eastern cliffs, I felt a sudden lurch of doubt. The cloud was so thick and the wind was becoming so strong I was unsure if I would even find the summit, let alone the remote area of hillside that held the Oxford's wreckage. What was it that Hamish Brown had observed about this part of the Cairngorms when on his epic, continuous completion of the Munros? 'North from here is some of the emptiest landscape in Britain. Go astray and you will go twenty miles possibly before seeing a habitation.' To lose my way in this place, I decided, would have serious consequences.

Eventually I found the cairn, by luck more than judgement, stumbling across it almost without realising, its grey outline gradually becoming more defined, until ten metres away I could make out the dark triangle of rocks that marked the otherwise indeterminate summit of Beinn a' Bhuird.

I sat with my back against the wet boulders and ate more chocolate. From this point onwards, route finding would become even more difficult. I planned to navigate in stages, at first taking a bearing to the head of an unnamed burn, then pacing out the distance to the cliffs of Garbh Choire, before redirecting my steps towards the thin promontory of land that marked the Stob an t-Sluichd spur.

Within a quarter of an hour of walking, however, I started to feel lost. I had not reached the burn I was searching for, and a slow tide of panic began to rise from my stomach. Perhaps I had missed it? A myriad of possibilities occurred to me. Perhaps my bearing had been out, or I had drifted off course? Maybe my distancing had been incorrect or the cairn was a false summit? Now everything seemed wrong.

I searched for answers in the visible landscape: subtle variations in gradient and slope that I hoped would match the contours on my map. There were no clues, no obvious signs. In the clouds the terrain seemed limitless, anonymous – a continuing, terrifying unknown. I would never find the Oxford in such conditions, I knew that. Suddenly, all I wanted to do was to find the way home.

———

I had felt chastened after my time on Beinn a' Bhuird, reminded sharply of the mountain's remoteness and my own vulnerabilities within that wild, extending space: walking blindly, bizarrely lost in the brightness, and moving against a wind so fierce it hampered my every movement. Eventually I had descended, of course. But for a while I had understood something of the imperceptible boundaries between safety and peril.

It was hardly a unique feeling. Anyone who has spent time on Britain's mountains will be familiar with the uncertainty and alarm of such moments, no matter how fleeting. It was in 'these Places', as the mountain-going poet, Samuel Taylor Coleridge declared, that we find somewhere not only physically, but spiritually 'lonely and savage and full of sounds'. Mine was an experience that had been played out by others on countless occasions, re-enacted to a greater or lesser degree a multitude of times every season in the Cairngorms and the mountains of Scotland.

Yet within its modern context my journey had been psychologically informed by the histories of those who had rescued, and who had been rescued in these mountains. I was, whether I realised it or not, the unwitting beneficiary of a substantial mountaineering legacy, the inheritor of decades of history of adventure and misadventure in Scotland's high places.

To head into the Cairngorms even a century ago would have been a vastly more serious undertaking than it is today. For a start, access to the mountains was much more restricted, road networks were less extensive; private as well as public transport was comparatively scarce; and leisure time significantly more limited than is the case today. Once in the Cairngorms, reaching any of the summits would have also required considerable commitment. Mountain-goers at the turn of the twentieth century operated within a narrow band of comfort and security. Functional limitations in clothing and equipment, in communications and knowledge, were both a hardship and a risk appreciably greater than that experienced by modern mountaineers.

Likewise, the mechanisms of rescue were still desperately inadequate. In his book *The Black Cloud*, the writer Ian Thomson adroitly summarises the dauntless, but primitive assistance that existed in Scotland at the time:

Search parties were largely dependent on those with local knowledge through their work on the moors and uplands: stalkers, gamekeepers, ghillies and shepherds with their dogs who with remarkable willingness went out, wearing ordinary clothes and footwear, sometimes in the most appalling of weather and at peril to their own lives, to search for an injured or missing mountaineer. The only equipment they carried that might be of assistance in finding the missing person was a stick or a crock and a telescope; their only means of communicating with each other was a shout, a whistle or a wave of a handkerchief; their only means of contacting their base was to dispatch one of their number on foot; and their only means of carrying the injured or dead was a pony or a stretcher, as often as not constructed on the spot from crooks and staves.

It was not until the early 1930s that the first signs of a unified approach to mountain rescue in Britain began to develop, prompted in particular by a now infamous incident in the Peak District.

Edgar Pryor had been climbing 'Long Climb' at Laddow, when he was knocked from his stance by a climber falling from above. Pryor dropped 15 metres into a neighbouring gully, fracturing his skull and breaking his leg. An *ad hoc* rescue mission was mounted: a splint was fashioned from a rucksack frame and a stretcher was improvised from the fingerpost of a nearby path. Pryor was then carried by a relay of stretcher bearers for over four hours to the nearest point an ambulance was able to reach. It was a further hour and a half before he reached Manchester Royal Infirmary. The journey was agonising and medically traumatic, later resulting in amputation of Pryor's leg.

The prolonged, excruciating nature of Pryor's journey to hospital and other similarly harrowing episodes led to a collaboration between two of the most important climbing clubs at the time. In 1932, the Rucksack Club and the Fell & Rock Climbing Club formed the 'Joint Stretcher Committee', a group tasked with finding the most efficient means of transporting casualties from the mountains. The committee soon agreed on a design, and 'Thomas Stretchers' were left at mountain rescue posts along with other essential first-aid equipment.

By 1936, a more permanent structure for the committee was in place, drawing funds from its various affiliated climbing clubs and changing its name to the 'First Aid Committee of Mountaineering Clubs'. More importantly, though, it had established a framework for an organisation that would eventually encompass the many individual civilian rescue teams that were to come into existence over the next thirty years in England and Wales. It was during this period also that a separate, distinctive evolution in Britain's mountain rescue provision occurred, arising not from recreational misfortune, but from wartime operations.

In a similar way to the civilian rescue efforts at the time, the RAF mountain rescue service developed not from a centralised leadership structure but from individual moral initiatives. Remarkably, until late in the Second World War there had been no official provision for the recovery of the hundreds of aircrew downed on Britain's high ground. Instead, scratch teams were assembled from local RAF bases, comprised quite simply of anyone available to assist when planes crashed in the locality. The *ad hoc* groups were often pitifully ill-equipped for the task. Few, if any, of the would-be rescuers had any mountaineering experience, and only the most standard of military equipment was provided. Searching large areas of wild landscape for survivors, as well as the inevitable recovery of bodies and wreckage over long distances and hard terrain, turned out to be a highly specialist job.

The Oxford crash on Beinn a' Bhuird was a case in point. Although there were no survivors, the height and the remoteness of the crash site meant that retrieving the bodies of the five airmen was a logistically complex and arduous undertaking. The whole operation lasted well over a week, required dozens of men and even involved the use of mules. It was, though, for precisely this type of incident, and the many others like it, that the RAF mountain rescue service was created.

To work in such an unforgiving environment required expertise and training, a fact that soon became recognised by personnel at various RAF bases across the country during the war. None more so than by Flt Lt George Graham, whose revolutionary ideas and determined lobbying eventually secured funding for an official RAF mountain rescue service in 1943. It was from these individual efforts that the RAF was soon able to set in place a template for mountain rescue. Civilian rescue teams soon followed suit. Regular training programmes, specialised equipment, standard operating procedures and a pool of permanent members became the norm.

By the early 1960s, mountain rescue in Britain had been radically transformed. In the Cairngorms, events such as the Oxford crash and many other aviation tragedies, as well as the Beinn a' Bhuird avalanche of 1964, proved that a growing number of accidents in the range could no longer be resolved by self-reliance and impromptu rescue alone. The formation of the Cairngorm Mountain Rescue Team (based in Aviemore) in 1963 and the Braemar Mountain Rescue Team in 1965 were the beginnings of a formalised response to accidents in the range. Their inception signified both conclusion and continuity; they represented the achievement of innumerable, previous acts of selflessness and the perpetuation of the traditions of volunteer rescue in the Cairngorms.

—

I had to wait before returning to Beinn a' Bhuird, biding my time through late autumn, winter and then spring. To search for the Oxford during this period would have been futile. The wreckage would be all but invisible until the early summer sun had burned back the concealing blanket of snow from the high plateau.

Predictably, though, the day I returned mirrored my initial journey. Cloud swathed the tops and a fine mist turned first to sleet and then to snow. By the time I had reached Stob an t-Sluichd the cloud had thickened, diffusing the light to an obscuring milky grey and once again limiting my field of vision to only a few dozen metres in every direction. This time, however, I was better prepared. I carried with me a grid reference for the Oxford, and, more importantly, a GPS device.

It wasn't long before I spotted what I had been looking for. An out-of-place shape: thin, crooked and upright in form, dark against the near horizon. As I moved closer, the wreckage became clear. Scattered on open ground, beneath a low spine of rocks, I saw metal: shards, mostly, thin, insubstantial and pocket-sized, lying strewn across a broad area of grass and boulders. The debris had a strangely animal quality: brutal and immediate, remains showing traces of violence like the stripped carcase of a raptor's quarry.

Several larger fragments caught my eye: machine blocks, functional in composition with rivets, bolts and circular openings. It was precision engineering, now static, but purposefully shaped and efficient. I sensed a memory of movement in the pieces, despite the welding scabs of rust, of parts interlocking, sliding and rotating, of metal once working fast against metal.

Within minutes of my arrival the sky had darkened. The light began closing in with all the murky speed of a midwinter's evening. Then snow fell faster and thicker. Large wet flakes melted into my jacket as soon as they landed and I had the irrational feeling that my presence there had somehow been acknowledged.

I saw the engines last. Two large turbines lying face down within metres of each other. Their outer casings had peeled off and the inner workings were visible, opened up to view like a mechanical dissection. Pipes and tubing radiated outwards, forming a seven-pointed star with mountings of layered steel, placed in neat lines resembling gills. The metal inside was matt-grey and black with intricate mouldings and skeletal connections. It had remained eerily uncorroded, seemingly unaffected by the high-altitude extremities, as if only a few years old.

I wondered grimly at the engines' placement. Such was their weight and their bulk that their present position must have been their original point of landing. They could not have moved since the crash – since the final moments of their halted momentum. The thought triggered in me a visceral reaction. I felt suddenly nauseous, abruptly aware of the latent energy of the place.

After waiting months to find the Oxford, I ended up staying only minutes. The wreckage and its isolation were abject and somehow sacrosanct. Each footstep seemed like an intrusion of sorts and I suddenly felt compelled to leave.

As I walked away, I noticed a small plaque on a flat section of a nearby boulder, discreetly placed and facing out onto the remains of the Oxford. 'To commemorate the supreme sacrifice' it read, 'of those aircrew of the Royal Air Force and their allies of World War II and in subsequent years who were killed flying in these mountains.' At the base of the boulder a small wooden cross had been placed unobtrusively and anonymously beneath the plaque. I had not seen another person in all the time that I had been on Beinn a' Bhuird, but someone else had also made the same deliberate journey as me, and in that remote and isolated place it seemed like a powerful act of remembrance.

Cairngorm Stone

'Civilization and fever . . . has not dimmed my glacial eye.'

John Muir.

My journeys in the Cairngorms had so far been precise, explorations to specific, often obscure points within the range in search of its secret histories. The routes had been deliberate and exact, if at times uncertain in their outcome: the trailing of the River Dee to locate the Wells of Dee, the hunt for Landseer's wilderness hideaway, the pilgrimage to the El Alamein refuge and the expedition for the Oxford wreckage all had a defined point of destination, a tangible location within the massif.

Yet there were secrets that also existed on a larger scale, too pervasive to be determined by a single set of coordinates, too ubiquitous not to be noticed, but easily overlooked or unacknowledged. They were the geological characteristics that made the Cairngorms unique: from the thrusting intrusions of granite that formed the range to the glacial scars that now defined the landscape. To understand the forms and shapes of the range, to interpret the signs of its creation, would be to understand a hidden history and an ongoing process: the formation and the reformation of the mountains of the Cairngorms.

No one, single journey in the Cairngorms could adequately encompass every aspect of its diverse landforms, but there was one geological feature of the range, more than any other, I was eager to see up close. The Cairngorm tors can seen rising from numerous summits in the range. I had seen them distantly on many occasions. From afar the strange protuberances spaced out across empty ridgelines of the plateau, in particular those of Bynack More and Beinn Mheadhoin, appeared deliberately formed: crumbling fortifications or wartime pill-boxes, long-deserted lodgings or the decaying follies of an eccentric. In the first Scottish Mountaineering Club guide to the range, Sir Henry Alexander described them as 'gigantic warts'. 'The rough crystalline granite,' Alexander explained, 'has in many cases weathered into horizontal slabs, so well defined and so regular as to give the impression of titanic masonry'.

One of the best places in the Cairngorms to encounter these geological oddities, however, was once again one of the most remote. Alexander pronounced the tors of Ben Avon as being 'far more numerous and more striking' than those on other mountains in the range, 'while the group of rocks on the north slope of Ben Avon known as the Clach Bun Rudhtair or the Needles, equals, if it does not surpass, the famous Barns of Bynack in magnitude and impressiveness'.

There was also another reason to reach Ben Avon. The mountain was once one of the prime places where the semi-precious gem that takes its name from the place of its one-time abundance was to be found. Cairngorm Stone had been mined extensively on Ben Avon from the eighteenth century onwards and now few pieces of the smoky quartz remain. Evidence of the gem mines, however, apparently still existed and I was keen to search for their presence on the mountain. A journey to Ben Avon and a search for Cairngorm Stone would also be an exploration of Cairngorm's stone and the unique events that have shaped the plateau.

Any passage through the Cairngorms, no matter how brief, requires an implicit or explicit deference to geology, a conscious or subconscious acknowledgement that a route must follow, or be determined by, landforms created over thousands, sometimes millions of years ago; movement across valley, corrie or summit is, after all, only made possible here by the turmoil of ancient volcanic cataclysm or by millennia of glacial action.

My route to Ben Avon, the most remote Munro in the Cairngorms, followed a similar line of geological influence. The few established paths that access its summit follow comparable lines of least resistance. From the north, the mountain is reached from the village of Tomintoul, trailing the River Avon through kilometres of a narrow defile. Likewise, the journey on foot from the east tracks the wide flood plain of the River Don. I chose to approach from the south, making my way inwards along Gleann an t-Slugain.

The glen has long been a passageway into the Cairngorms. It is a shallow cleft in the landscape that for centuries has served as a natural corridor and an ancient right of way. In its upper reaches the glen changes shape, its slopes steepen and converge, funnelling towards a miniature gorge flanked with small saplings in its rock walls: birch, rowan and alder.

The glen's name is fitting. Slugain roughly translates from the Gaelic for gullet, a suitable reference to the enclosed climb through the thin neck of the ravine. I followed a path that passed between crumbling rock-walls of granite, walking in what was once a torrential subterranean riverbed.

Upper Gleann an t-Slugain was formed as the glaciers of the Cairngorms receded. Huge volumes of water were released with the retreating ice, creating a river that flowed under the glacier and which was powerful enough to cleave a deep incision into the underlying bedrock. The result today is the remains of a 'meltwater channel', a narrow boulder-strewn opening that has its familial counterparts throughout the Cairngorms and the rest of Scotland.

In the upper glen, I came across the ruins of a building. Slugain Lodge had been built for Victorian shooting parties as a stopping-off point to and from the wider reaches of the range, but had been abandoned in the early twentieth century. It was clearly once a redoubtable structure. The remaining walls were deep and large blocks of its granite masonry lay spread at the foot of the building.

Until 1944, there had also been another building in this part of the glen. The wooden Slugain Bothy had stood only 100 yards further up from the Lodge and was a popular base for climbers until its untimely demise. The story goes that the bothy had been deliberately destroyed, burnt down after the estate factor had discovered items there, stolen from a cottage near Invercauld. It was perhaps the removal of the Slugain Bothy, however, that prompted the construction of the Cairngorms' most elusive buildings.

The secret howffs of Upper Gleann an t-Slugain were perfectly situated. Built by climbers from Aberdeen to gain easy access to the corries of Beinn a' Bhuird, the shelters also took advantage of the natural geology of the glen, its seclusion and its hiding places. 'The construction is partly subterranean', the famous Aberdonian climber Tom Patey once explained about one of the buildings, 'and is the eighth wonder of the Cairngorms, with a stove, floorboards, genuine glass window and seating space for six . . . It stood in a small village of howffs, three in number and together capable of accommodating an entire climbing meet.'

Such was the clandestine nature of the building of the howffs that 'materials were brought from Aberdeen to the assembly line by the Herculean labours of countless torchlit safaris which trod stealthily past the Laird's very door, shouldering mighty beams of timber, sections of stove piping and sheets of corrugated iron'. The howffs were elaborate but remained well concealed. So much so that at one point, one of the intended residents fell through a skylight, 'deceived by the almost foolproof camouflage.'

Further up, at the head of the glen, the topography changed once more, opening up into a grassy clearing with a small lozenge-shaped lochan in its centre. The place felt still and unseen; sunk down below the breezes that whipped across the surrounding moorland and bordered on every side by tawny heather. The bright green of the clearing seemed out of place; verdant and incongruous in its surroundings, an unexpected and mysterious glade. Locals refer to this part of Gleann an t-Slugain as the Fairy Glen, the geology lending itself easily to mysticism; a place of myths and storytelling for those who pass through it.

Cairngorm place-names are imbued with significance, yet the modern name of the range itself is misleading. The etymology is simple but relatively recent in its derivation. In his authoritative book, *Scottish Hill Names*, Peter

Drummond explains the difference between the ancient and the contemporary ways of referring to the massif. 'In Gaelic the range is known as Am Monadh Ruadh, the red-mountain land, from the pink colour of the granite that composes them. It became known universally in English as the Cairngorms in the last century, taking the name from this one rounded swell of a mountain that is prominent in the view from Speyside'.

The change in name was significant, for in its literal translation it also described a change in colour for the range: Cairn Gorm means the blue (or green) hill. The renaming was unintentionally symbolic. The transition from being red mountains (their colour when seen close-up, intimately), to blue mountains (their colour when seen from a distance, from the outside), marked a time of transition in the region: an encroachment of external influences, the gradual demise of the indigenous Gaelic culture and a departure from the oral traditions that had defined many of the features within the range.

The ancient names in the Cairngorms are signs of ritual and relationship, of geology fusing with human history, landforms as way-markers and record-keepers, the begetters of stories and the focal-points of legends, 'that show,' as Nan Shepherd had observed, 'how old is man's association with scaur and corrie: the Loch of the Thin Man's Son, the Coire of the Cobbler, the Dairymaid's Meadow, the Lurcher's Crag.'

As is the case in other mountainous areas of Britain, some of the most evocative and enduring names in the Cairngorms relate not to peaks or valleys, but to the smallest of geological features. Often they are too small to be recorded on maps, but are instead retained in local consciousness in recognition that they distinguish parts of a wild place, so that they are handed down and reused in direction-giving and storytelling: a waterfall perhaps, or the confluence of two streams, the brow of a hill, or, more often than not, the singular occurrence of a distinctive stone or rock formation.

There are several instances of these mineral landmarks in the Cairngorms, each with their own significance or notoriety. The writer Ian Murray has retold the story of the Clach Thogalach, or the 'Stone of the Lifting' that was once used as a challenge of strength for local men. The stone could, apparently, barely be lifted until one man outdid his peers with consummate ease, throwing the rock into the River Lui where it apparently rests to this day. High on the western side of Gleann Einich is the Argyll Stone, a pronounced outcrop of wind-rounded granite easily visible from across the glen. Legend has it that the stone takes its name from the Duke of Argyll, who in 1594 was sent to quell a rebellion of Catholic insurgents in Glenlivet. The Duke's forces were routed at the Battle of Allt na Coilleachan and he was harried south in retreat, briefly resting with his troops at the rocks that now bear his name.

Perhaps my favourite merging of geology and myth in the Cairngorms relates to a set of stones that I have passed by on several occasions. The Clach nan Taillear, or 'Tailors' Stones', are a group of large, table-topped rocks lying just off the main path in the Lairig Ghru, roughly one kilometre from the Corrour Bothy. The story of the rocks is well known, but like all great fables, historically unproven.

One Hogmanay three tailors from Abernethy boasted they could dance at three separate locations within a day. A drunken bet was made and they attempted to fulfil their wager, first by dancing at Abernethy and then at Rothie-murchus. To complete their task, however, they would also need to dance in Dalmore in Mar, on the southern side of the Lairig Ghru pass and a distance of over thirty kilometres away. As the inebriated tailors descended from the high point of the pass a ferocious storm blew in. By the time the men had made their way halfway through the valley, they were exhausted by their efforts and the weather, and seeking shelter amongst the rocks, the three tailors duly perished, thus bequeathing the landmark its name.

Whether fact or fiction, the story of the Tailors' Stones is an easily explained piece of local lore – its existence serving two separate purposes. On one level the naming of the stones renders them useful as a navigational aid; a noticeable reference point within the long stretch of the Lairig Ghru. On another level, however, the tale works as a salutary lesson; a fable cautioning against the dangers of the Cairngorm winter and warning others not to underestimate its ferocity.

The fates of the stones and the eponymous tailors are also fittingly analogous. The surfaces of the stones have a strangely corrugated appearance; striations etched deeply into the rock in parallel grooves and ridges. The patterns are the scars of grinding glacial action; evidence of the stones' own harrowing journey through the glen.

From the Fairy Glen I moved north, upwards and outwards into kilometres of moorland littered with glacial debris. I soon passed by a cluster of large triangular boulders, tilted at forty-five degrees from the ground. Their shapes continued down into the soil, submerging so that they resembled icebergs or the upturned bows of sinking ships.

Like the Tailors' Stones, these rocks were erratics, lifted and carried by glacial action until they were deposited by the melting ice sheets far from their original lithologic origins. Erratics can be found widely across the Cairngorms. In their smallest forms they are often scarcely noticeable, but larger specimens can appear spectacular and unmistakable, contrasting markedly with their surroundings or positioned in seemingly improbable locations.

I knew of several of these monolithic castaways. There was the large oblong boulder on the slopes of Creagan Gorm, standing almost upright like a sacred standing stone looking out towards the Northern Corries. Then there was the Clach Barraig, the huge block of granite that rests precariously above the road to the ski centre car park in Coire Cas. From below, the massive rock is silhouetted on the horizon, appearing as though it might tumble downhill at any moment. But perhaps the most spectacular of all Cairngorm erratics was one I had never seen. The Clach a' Cleirich sits near the junction of the Allt Dearg and Glas Allt Mor on the slopes of Ben Avon. The stone was so big and so distinctive that, I had been told, I couldn't miss it on my route to the tors.

The path towards Ben Avon was equally conspicuous. Pale and pink, it snaked across the dark moorland for several kilometres until it eventually disappeared from view, rounding the corner of a distant hillside. To my left, as I walked, I caught glimpses of the Quoich Water. Over time, the river has become embedded in the land around it, cutting a progression deeper and deeper so that it is barely visible within the glen. Near the river's wake, there were small terraces of flat ground; deltas of raised earth like small islands set amongst the heather. These too were the calling cards of glacial visitation.

The delta terraces had been formed during successive retreats of the Cairngorm glaciers. As the mountain ice-sheets thawed, they had separated from the larger valley glaciers of Strathspey, Deeside and Strathdon. Ice-dammed lakes were created as melt-water, trapped in the interior of the range, was unable to make its way past the surrounding valley glaciers. The shelves of flat ground I could see marked the levels of the ancient lakes and echoed a landform found more spectacularly in other parts of the range, most notably in Gleann Einich and the northern end of the Lairig Ghru.

At the head of the glen, the edges of the moor converged and a triptych of corries came into view. This was the sheer eastern face of Beinn a' Bhuird, the alter ego of the mountain's gently inclining western slopes: pleats of deep rock walls and buttresses extending in length, continuous and precipitous, for several dizzying kilometres. The corries provide some of the best climbing routes in the range, but their remoteness presented a problem to early mountaineers. The secret howffs in the Fairy Glen went some way to improving the access to the Beinn a' Bhuird climbs, but in 1948 an even nearer shelter was discovered below the Dividing Buttress between Coire an Dubh lochain and Coire nan Clach.

Two climbers, Mac Smith and Kenny Winram, had for some time harboured the ambition of finding their very own howff somewhere in the Cairngorms. On one particularly wet weekend, poor weather prevented climbing and prompted instead, a search of the Beinn a' Bhuird corries for a suitable natural shelter. The pair spent hours scouring the boulder-covered ground of the Coire nan Clach until Smith spotted a dark space under a large moraine boulder. 'I shouted to Winram, intent on searching his own allotted area,' wrote Smith in the *Cairngorm Club Journal*, describing the immediate, geological suitability of what he had found. 'He dashed across and together we advanced expectantly . . . It was it! Our spiritual home! Our Howff! In the damp dark atmosphere of the mist-laden corrie I must admit it did not look a prepossessing place at first glance. On closer inspection it improved. A large block lay on a smaller slab forming one straight wall, and a semi-circle of rubble and small blocks provided the other walls and further support. Much work would be needed to make it windproof. The ceiling was flat, a quartz-encrusted slab of pink unweathered granite standing about five feet above the floor.'

Cairngorm stone made the Smith-Winram howff possible. The shelter exploited the geology of the corries, a cave discovered amongst its fallen rocks. But the howff also shared a connection with the search for Cairngorm Stone: an association with one of Scotland's most famous climbers and an avid exponent of gem hunting in the range.

Mac Smith and Kenny Winram had been inspired to build their howff by an article in the *Scottish Mountaineering Club Journal* written by the legendary Glaswegian climber and shipyard worker, Jock Nimlin.

In *Mountain Howffs* Nimlin had extolled the virtues of finding rudimentary shelter in the geology of the mountains. 'They can be built on any hill where rock debris is plentiful,' Nimlin explained. 'Once built they are practically indestructible and the material for repairs is always at hand.' Nimlin also proposed that the use of howffs befitted an idealistic approach to time spent outdoors, realising a 'conformity with the primal nature of the mountain scene', concluding that their inherent close-ness to the environment 'is strictly in line with the ascetic nature of mountaineering'. 'Whilst living there,' Nimlin suggested in almost monastic tones, 'the climber accepts the austerity of mountain life . . . No other approach gives the climber such close communion with the hills.'

Nimlin's purest philosophy of mountaineering began at an early age and was to inform his life-long relationship with wild places. Like so many of Glasgow's dispossessed youth in the 1920s and '30s, Nimlin gravitated to the almost permanent campfire that burned at Craigallian Woods, just north of Glasgow. 'The Craigallian Fire was famous among the Glasgow weekenders, of whom there could be upwards of 30 sitting in its warm glow,' retells Ian Thomson, in his biography of Jock Nimlin, *May the Fire Always Be Lit*. 'During the depression, when there was so much unemployment and short-time working, some spent almost the entire week there, returning to the city only to collect their dole.'

The camaraderie, and in particular the immediacy of the natural environment that Nimlin experienced at the Craigallian Fire, were to leave a lasting impression on him: 'The setting, the wooded hollow with its ranks of varied trees reflecting the changing colours of the year on the sheltered loch, and the double echo, sensitive to the lightest bird-call epitomise the wonder of the wide Scottish landscapes...the other fires that were soon to burn in the woods and the howffs of the Highlands were projections of this parent.'

Nimlin became a pioneering climber and outdoors-man, completing numerous first ascents and founding the Ptarmigan Mountaineering Club – the very first working-class climbing club in Scotland. He later became the first warden for the National Trust for Scotland, a post he held for seventeen years.

The Cairngorms were of particular interest to Nimlin. He climbed extensively in the range and was a volunteer instructor at the then newly opened Outdoor Training Centre at Glenmore Lodge. But it was prospecting in the crystal-rich geology of the Cairngorms that fuelled his abiding lapidary passion. Nimlin was a recognised authority on the gemstones of Scotland and his encyclopaedic knowledge on the subject, amassed over years of close scrutiny of the natural environment, eventually found form in the small but accessible publication, *Let's Look at Scottish Gemstones*.

The work is endearing: part factual, part anecdotal. Nimlin's text reveals his specialism and his passion, combining the detail of an expert with the enthusiasm of a hobbyist. 'A careful scrutiny of even a small part of Scotland with its countless rock exposures, screes, stream beds, sea cliffs, and pebble beaches brings the realisation that a huge area awaits the detailed examination necessary to determine the true extent of the country's gemstone resources.'

Of all the areas mentioned in the booklet, the Cairngorms are referenced the most. Nimlin's knowledge of the unique geology of the range was extensive; from the locations of mineral-rich sites and ancient gem workings, through to the folklore that surrounded crystal hunting. He knew Cairngorm Stone like few others: its contradictory secret history and its ubiquitous but elusive quality – geology tending to myth. 'There are stories of fabulous finds.' Nimlin wrote, aware of the centuries-old lure of gem hunting in the Cairngorms. 'One legend is of a great "brilliant" which sometimes gleams from a precipice high above Loch Avon and defies all attempts to locate it.'

—

Understanding the creation of the Cairngorm range requires a fast-forwarding of time, a view of the mountains as if filmed as a set of time-lapse images. When imagined in this way the geological history of the range resembles a stop-motion recording: a movement through time and across the surface of the planet, uplifting from sea level, then falling, then rising again.

The mountains of the Cairngorms were formed during the monumental changes in the earth's crust between 488 to 444 million years ago. As the ancient continents of Baltica, Eastern Avalonia and Laurentia began to collide, oceanic sediments were compacted, buried and intensely heated. The metamorphosed Dalradian rock that resulted was then forced great distances upwards by the opposing tectonic forces to create a huge mountain range. The Caledonian Mountain Chain was massive in scale: Alpine, perhaps even Himalayan in size, and the geological forebear of today's Grampian Highlands, the mountains of Scandinavia and the Appalachian Mountains in North America.

It was during this momentous period of mountain building in the Caledonian Orogeny that Cairngorm granite was also formed. Deep below the earth's surface the transacting forces of continental collision superheated rock to a molten state. The resulting magma was lighter than the surrounding rocks and gradually seeped upwards. Vast capsules of this volcanic material cooled before ever reaching the surface, solidifying amongst the Dalradian sediment in colossal, underground plutons of granite.

The granite remained hidden for many millions of years, secreted deep within the Caledonian mountains, until intense weathering and erosion during the Devonian Period, between 416 and 359 million years ago, stripped back much of the surrounding Dalradian rock, grinding down the mountains and exposing the more erosion-resistant granite.

Over the following 200 million years, the land we now know as Scotland moved gradually northwards above the equator. During this time the Cairngorms were an area of high ground surrounded by arid continental plains and desert sands. By the Cretaceous Period, 146 to 65 million years ago, the height of the Cairngorms had dramatically reduced, rising barely above the warm sea waters that covered most of Scotland.

Much of the Cairngorms' present-day appearance, however, can be traced from the Palaeogene Period onwards. Around 65 million years ago a rapid uplift of the Highlands re-established the Cairngorms as an upland area. Meanwhile, warm global temperatures created a humid, subtropical climate in Scotland causing significant chemical weathering of the Cairngorm granite. In these conditions the Cairngorm landforms familiar today were formed: glens were eroded along lines of weakness in the rock and the elevation of low-relief areas produced the whale-backed summits and sweeping stretches of the plateau. The Ice Age was to follow of course, glaciers advancing and retreating, effortlessly sculpting the landscape.

I saw it almost immediately, rising perpendicular from the ground, its sides smooth and angular, converging at the top like an oblong pyramid. It was true, the Clach a' Cléirich was impossible to miss: barely twenty metres from the path and standing well above my own height – solitary and prominent like a cultic monument or a prehistoric shrine. At the base of the rock, the heather of the surrounding slopes petered out and was replaced by a two-metre radius of short grass: a small processional circuit – inviting, or caused by, repetitions of footfall.

I paced slowly around the grassy loop. As I did so, the erratic's angles and height appeared differently. It no longer stood vertical as I had first thought, but slanted diagonally in an improbable overhang, its weight some-how cantilevered upwards from beneath the soil. I could think of few other landmarks in the Cairngorms that were so distinctive, so conspicuous in their surroundings. Even its name was memorable. Clach a' Cleirich translated as the Priest's Stone. Like the Tailors of the Lairig Ghru, the titular clergyman was also lost to modern records, unac-countable in history, but now woven into the cultural memory of the landscape.

From the stone I moved upwards, treading a steady incline, on the remote but well used ascent to Ben Avon. On the steep slopes on either side I saw yet more huge erratics. One in particular caught my eye. It was massive and spectacularly incongruent, a huge wedge of rectan-gular granite sliced cleanly on each of its sides, battleship grey and lying flat against the grass.

After half an hour the path ended abruptly, cresting on an area of flat, boulder-clad ground. I was standing on the Sneck – a narrow mountain isthmus joining the two island massifs of Beinn a' Bhuird and Ben Avon. A wide vista opened up on the other side of the saddle: a previously unseen valley several kilometres long, deep and pathless. Such unexpected views in the Cairngorm mountains can be breathtaking. 'The change in scene once the Sneck is reached is startling,' Henry Alexander wrote admiringly. 'After having come for a mile or more up a grassy glen with not unfriendly hillsides on either hand, one finds oneself suddenly on a sharp and craggy edge gazing down into one of the wildest corries in the Cairngorms.'

From the surrounding peaks mist poured into the hidden glen. I watched a small squall form at the entrance to the valley: a churning bundle of cloud that snowballed in size as it bowled towards me. It arrived like a sandstorm: a sudden blast of wind and ice particles that stung my face. I found shelter behind one of the large granite boulders and watched bright hailstones fire past me like tracer bullets.

The storm passed quickly, moving southwards and leaving patches of blue sky in its wake. I continued upwards from the Sneck on a switchback path of loose pink scree to reach the summit plateau of Ben Avon where I hoped to begin my search for Cairngorm Stone.

There was little hope that my untrained eye would locate the tell-tale signs of the semi-precious crystal deposits – the scatterings or seams of milky quartz disappearing beneath the surface-level of the plateau – and there was even less chance of me finding any uncollected specimens. But evidence still remained of gem hunting on Ben Avon: excavations and spoil heaps, now barely noticeable, but clearly still pock-marking the surface of the Cairngorm mountains centuries later.

One of the earliest written records of the practice of crystal foraging in the Cairngorms dates back to the end of the eighteenth century. The *Statistical Account* of

1791–99 refers to 'Stones of value', to be found, 'sometimes by chance or accident; at other times by digging for them' near the Shelter Stone in Loch Avon. The language of the account suggests a well-established interest in gem hunting in the region, reporting a 'number of stones of variegated colours, and regular sides' appearing, 'as if cut by the lapidary'.

The surge in popularity of private crystal collections from the mid-eighteenth century onwards created a demand for semi-precious stones not only from home but also from mainland Europe. Cairngorm Stone in particular was much sought after. With the increased demand came a marketable value and the search for crystals in the range suddenly became a profitable undertaking.

For the most part, the crystal hunters of the Cairngorms were local people, shepherds and stalkers, well used to the rigours of life in the hills. Like their mountain-dwelling counterparts in the Alps they would turn their hand, or rather their eye, to finding gemstones during their daytime occupations, chancing upon finds or occasionally working known deposits in the more remote areas of their daily travels.

A cottage industry for retrieving Cairngorm Stone, however, soon came into being. Prospectors mined sites across the range, in particular high on the summit plateaus of Beinn Mheadhoin, Cairn Gorm, Beinn a' Bhuird and Ben Avon. Likely veins of quartz were dug back into the soil, faults and ancient gas cavities in the bedrock were exposed and blasted out. The resulting depressions in the surface of the plateau from these more industrial searches can still be seen today.

Some incredible finds were made. The largest crystal discovered was a huge piece of beryl weighing over 50lbs.

Fittingly it was unearthed on Beinn a' Bhuird by perhaps the most prolific of all the Cairngorm gem hunters, a crystal prospector known as 'A'Chailleach nan Clach', the Old Woman of the Stones.

Numerous types of gemstones have been found throughout the Cairngorms. Of all the crystals present, quartz is by far the most abundant. Milky quartz can be seen almost everywhere in the range, scattered like rock salt or ice clusters or running through stones and rocks in lucent white stripes, banding and partitioning the granite. Clear quartz (known as rock crystal); yellow (known as citrine) and dense black varieties (known as morion) can also be found. The term 'Cairngorm', although often generically used for any gemstone from the range, refers specifically to the particular type of smoky brown quartz, once so plentiful it became synonymous with the mountains.

Beryl has also been collected in various different shades: heliodor (gold/yellow); aquamarine (pale) and emerald (green). As has topaz, differing notably from its usual spectrum of colourless to yellow tones and discovered in striking blue hues in the Cairngorms.

Gemstones are now seldom found in the Cairngorms without a deliberate search or expert knowledge. Centuries of collecting as curiosities or latterly for profit or as a hobby have stripped all but the most obscure of the range's mineral treasures. Finds such as those recorded by Queen Victoria in 1850, where the monarch and her party 'came upon a number of "cairngorms"' in Gleann Slugain seem highly unlikely today. So too does the spectacular find told of by the naturalist Seton Gordon in his 1912 book *The Charm of the Hills*.

Gordon describes an expedition to an unnamed and 'out-of-the-way' corrie in Cairngorms; a place so remote that, 'probably not a single human being had penetrated [there] during the last century.'

While measuring and photographing a snow-field, Gordon and his companions notice 'a vein of quartz running up the rock immediately above the snow'. On closer examination of the vein they discovered 'embedded in the rocks . . . the points of some very fine cairngorms.' The stones were 'sherry-coloured' and of exceptional quality. In an age that pre-dated the contemporary awareness of protecting geodiversity and spurred on by their find they resolved to move a nearby rock in search of more of the gemstones. After two hours' work, they managed to dislodge the boulder, sending it 'roaring down into the snow beneath'. What they then unearthed was a gem hunter's dream: 'Sure enough, in the clay exposed by the departure of the stone numbers of cairngorms were found. They were of various sizes and shapes, but not a few of them were perfectly formed and scarcely without a flaw.' The group eventually retraced their steps back out of the corrie, carrying with them 'a rich haul of stones'.

———

I walked in transects on the Ben Avon plateau, methodically splitting the grid squares on my map into imaginary halves and quarters, prospecting for signs of crystals. My method was simple but speculative. By searching systematically, dividing the terrain into a series of sections, I hoped to narrow my chances of spotting the inconspicuous disturbances of ground that indicated the once active gem mines.

By early afternoon I had tramped the geometric equivalent of several kilometres. I had seen nothing that resembled crystal workings and the land was beginning to blur around me. I temporarily gave up, acknowledging both the intricacy of the search and the enormity of the plateau. I moved north, certain instead of encountering some of the Cairngorm's most characteristic features.

The summit tor of Ben Avon came into view suddenly, curling upwards on the skyline like a breaking wave. Mist had descended, moving in patches, closing and then opening the horizon. Leabaidh an Daimh Bhuidhe was the highest point on the mountain but it appeared only briefly, flickering through the cloud-breaks, the first in the chain of tors running south to north along the Ben Avon plateau.

Up close, the tor was incredible: a large battlement of wet-black granite, at least thirty metres long and almost ten metres high. The rock appeared almost organic in form: bulbous and wind-rounded, moulded over the millennia into something resembling mutated, biological shapes. When I looked for more than a few moments, I saw faces and limbs. Contorted expressions, figureheads, gargoyles and monsters; inanimate but grotesque and gothic in their appearance.

I scrambled up a gap in the midpoint of the tor. Despite the dampness, the rocks felt coarse and abrasive, rasping at my fingertips, and I was able to clamber easily along the narrow band of granite to the top of the feature. From the summit I looked northwards. By now, the cloud was lifting, being burned back by the sun, evaporating from the ground in wisps and flumes like steam rising from a bath.

The view had a massive visual scale. It felt cinematic: an epic horizon like the opening credits of a David Lean film. A path scrolled out ahead of me, eventually fading into the middle distance. Across the plateau I could see other tors emerging from the mist: dark, maritime shapes, spectral galleons held up on the rolling levels of the land.

Each of the tors differed markedly in size and shape, from small clusters to huge edifices of rock, some the size of houses. To the northeast just over a kilometre away I spotted a perfectly symmetrical tor. It was large and dome-like, and from a distance resembled a mausoleum or a giant termite mound.

Walking north from Leabaidh an Daimh Bhuidhe the upper world of Ben Avon assumed a fantastical reality, a landscape abstracted from the normality of sea-level topography. I passed by huge walls of granite, sculpted with extravagant curves and sweeping lines. There were embankments of blancmange-shaped rock, puffy and soft-edged, and clutches of boulders, smooth and time-rounded, the size of dinosaur eggs.

The largest and most bizarre of Ben Avon's dreamlike features lies on a northern spur of the plateau. Clach Bun Rudhtair has no geological equal in Britain. It is one of the largest of the Cairngorm tors and the most spectacular; a geological oddity of immense proportions. Rising twenty-five metres from the ground in columns of seal-grey granite, Clach Bun Rudhtair is almost impossible to comprehend. Its scale and form seem preternatural, evoking Dali-esque imagery or unexplained, ancient human constructions – Neolithic dolmens or the Moai statues of the Easter Islands.

To walk on the Ben Avon plateau, among such strange rock formations, is not only a journey through the surreal, but a voyage in a disentombed landscape. That afternoon I walked amongst the geology of the disinterred, rock-forms that had been uncovered through thousands of years of gradual exhumation.

The creation of the tors began during pre-glacial times. Chemical weathering of the granite exploited uneven densities in the rock, decomposing the more densely fractured areas of the plateau, but leaving other areas comparatively undamaged. As the processes of weathering continued during the milder phases of the Quaternary the weaker, more rotten granite was stripped away, leaving behind only the most solid concentrations of rock – our modern day tors.

Such landforms, although peculiar, are not unique to the Cairngorms. In Britain, they have their granite counterparts most notably on Bodmin Moor and Dartmoor. Geological parallels also exist in other parts of the world; eroded rock features such as monadnocks, inselbergs, bornhardts, nubbins and kopjes share a similar genesis. Where they occur, a cultural or psychogeological importance is often assigned to such anomalies in the landscape. On the northern slopes of Ben Avon, one tor in particular attracted just such a specific ritual significance.

Clach Bhan, literally meaning the Stone of the Women, is situated at a height of over 800 metres in one of the most inaccessible corners of the range. The summit surface of the tor is extraordinary. The grinding, circular action of stone fragments has, over thousands of years, created deep potholes in the granite, which, when filled with rainwater, resemble large, coastal rock pools.

The peculiarity of the Clach Bhan tor and its water-filled summit spawned a superstition that was gruelling in its fulfilment. Legend had it that pregnant women who were prepared to make the long and arduous journey to Clach Bhan, climb the precarious granite walls of the tor and bathe in its icy-cold potholes would, after all of that, experience an easier labour in childbirth.

Looking into Garbh Choire Mòr, home to Scotland's perpetual snow.

The interior of Ruigh-aiteachain bothy.

The two engines of the Oxford Mk I on a remote northern spur of
Beinn a' Bhuird.

The Shelter Stone Crag and Cairn Etchachan.

The Shelter Stone. The entrance to the cave is to the right of the pile of small stones in the centre.

The path between Ben Macdui and Loch Etchachan.

Looking down on the El Alamein Refuge and the steep slopes of Strath Nethy.

The Sneck and the cloud-covered plateau of Beinn a' Bhuird.

A small stone tablet, once part of the St Valery refuge and inscribed with it name, near the original position of the refuge above the cliffs of Stag Rock

The Sappers' Bothy near the summit of Ben Macdui.

The surreal granite tors on the vast expanse of the Ben Avon plateau.

Looking south into the wide breach of the Lairig Ghru from Braeriach.

The Cat's Den Cave in the heart of Rothiemurchus.

Cairngorm Stone

It is strange to think of mere rock-forms possessing spiritual or talismanic powers. Yet the geology of the Cairngorms exerts a potent imaginative magnetism. The search for gemstones; the veneration of erratics and naming of stones; Smith and Winram's quest for the perfect howff, all reveal a deep but subconscious reverence. An unwitting homage, still resonant today in small but meaningful acts: a stone placed on a summit cairn or a palm pressed flat against a cold rock-face.

Cairngorm Stone eluded me on Ben Avon. I found no sign of gemstones as I paced out the confusing groundscape of the plateau. Not that I was surprised. The absence of Cairngorm Stone now formed part of its own secret history: a kind of negative evidence. Proof, undoubtedly, not only of the centuries of human interest in the mineral content of the range, but also demonstrating an alternative way of looking at the Cairngorm landscape that observes the intricate detail as well as the manifest geology of the mountains. It is an acknowledgement that a single rock-face can hold as much wonder as an entire corrie or glen, and it reminded me of a passage I had read in the first SMC district guide to the range.

'The first fleeting impression made by these mountains may be one of disappointment,' Henry Alexander had observed, 'but, as one explores them and wanders among them, the magnitude of everything begins to reveal itself, one realizes the immensity of the scale upon which the scene is set.'

The Big Grey Man

'Who is the third who walks always beside you?
When I count, there are only you and I together.'
T. S. Eliot, *The Wasteland*.

'I was returning from the cairn on the summit in a mist when I began to think I heard something else than merely the noise of my own footsteps.' In 1925, Professor J. Norman Collie gave voice to an unexplained experience that many visitors to the Cairngorms have since also claimed to have had.

Collie was addressing the 27th Annual General Meeting of the Cairngorm Club when he first spoke of his supernatural encounter on Ben Macdui, thirty-five years earlier.

> Every few steps I took I heard a crunch, then another crunch as if someone was walking after me but taking steps three or four times the length of my own. I said to myself 'this is all nonsense'. I listened and heard it again but could see nothing in the mist. As I walked on and the eerie crunch, crunch sounded behind me I was seized with terror and took to my heels, staggering blindly among the boulders for four or five miles nearly down to Rothiemurchus Forest. Whatever you make of it I do not know, but there is something very queer about the top of Ben MacDhui and I will not go back there again by myself I know.

The account is now the stuff of mountaineering legend: an unidentifiable presence in a high and remote place; the lone summiteer being tracked through the mist; unreserved fear and a retreat from the mountain. The quote, though, is beguiling, a confusing mix of the theatrical and the plausible. Part campfire yarn, part credible witness statement, far-fetched but sincerely delivered, an account that gained an instant and enduring notoriety.

I had ascended Ben Macdui on many occasions. I knew of its broad open summit and its expansive views; its propensity towards extreme weather and its capacity to stage sudden and violent storms. I also knew of its mystery: the legacy of Collie's famous quote and the dozens of other similar descriptions that compound the mountain's reputation for ghostly, unexplained occurrences.

Depending on the precise version you choose to believe, the mountain is either haunted, or inhabited, by the Big Grey Man – or Am Fear Liath Mór in its Gaelic rendition. Accounts vary in their description. In its physical form, the Grey Man is popularly described as a giant, yeti-like creature, stalking the hillside, often in conditions of mist and snow.

More frequently, though, reports of the phenomenon involve a metaphysical dimension. An indefinable sensation of terror or dread is encountered near the summit. In Affleck Gray's definitive book on the Grey Man, he retells the experience of the Mountain Rescue team leader, Peter Densham.

On a clear day in May 1945, Densham had reached the summit of Ben Macdui and was alone when mist closed in. 'I had the sudden impression there was someone near me,' Densham recounted; at first dismissing the feeling as 'an impression which is sometimes experienced by mountaineers'. He then noticed the temperature drop sharply and became 'conscious of a crunching noise from the direction of the cairn.' As he moved towards the sound, Densham reported being suddenly 'overcome by a feeling of apprehension,' and as in the Collie account, felt immediately compelled to leave the mountain, which he did, 'running at incredible pace', not stopping for several miles until he reached Glenmore.

Myths however, are self-perpetuating. Folklore can evolve exponentially from a particular incident or story, spawning a plethora of similar accounts, each with their own resonance. In this way Densham's narrative seems imitative, bearing more than a convenient similarity to Collie's description thirty years earlier.

But both stories are equally perplexing. Neither of the men were inexperienced mountain-goers. Far from it. Densham had been involved in aircraft rescue activities in the Cairngorms during the Second World War while Collie was one of the pre-eminent mountaineers of his generation. Each would have been accustomed to the solitude of remote places and the unpredictable conditions of the mountain environment. That men of such stout mountaineering pedigree could be seized with genuine fear in the same place was baffling. That the same experience, however, could be reported by other seasoned mountaineers, such the pioneering Himalayan explorer A. M. Kellas, was utterly intriguing.

I wanted to ascend Ben Macdui once again. Not with the expectation of encountering the Grey Man, but to understand more of the mountain itself; its topography and orography. To know if there was something unique that could be determined about Britain's second highest peak: a set of conditions that could perhaps translate or explain its myths.

By making an indirect journey to the mountain's summit I also hoped to fulfil two other Cairngorm ambitions. The first would be to walk by way of Strath Nethy, the steep-sided valley that I had stared down into during my search for the El Alamein Shelter. My maps indicated the dashed line of a path running the entire length of the glen and I was keen to explore a route that charted its hidden depths.

Secondly, I planned to stay the night at the Shelter Stone, the ancient cave beneath a giant rock-face in the heart of the Cairngorms. Through the centuries the place had harboured thieves, bandits, artists, politicians, wayfarers and climbers alike. To spend the night in such historic accommodation would be the ultimate rite of passage to the range.

Strath Nethy is one of the most enigmatic of the Cairngorm glens. Most guidebooks are succinct in their description of it and the majority of nearby routes skirt around or above it. Viewed from height, as it most often is, the valley is strikingly linear; a long glacial trough extending without deviation for over seven kilometres. Its flanks are steep and boulder-strewn and the narrow valley floor remains hidden from sight. It is an area of the Cairngorms frequently seen but rarely ventured through. A place, in both senses of the word, overlooked.

Within minutes of leaving the deserted car-park at Coire na Ciste the path that was so clearly marked on my map had vanished. Ankle-deep heather soon reached knee-height, crowding out the muddy track and swallowing it up. My route into Strath Nethy had abruptly ended after five minutes, melting into acres of blank moorland.

A steady drizzle gathered, clouding the foreground and falling in droplets from the rim of my hood. I pressed on with tangled strides, following the path's imagined line in the landscape.

After an hour I reached woodland. My trousers and boots were sodden and I sank down against the trunk of a pine, relieved to have got the worst of the walk out the way. The path would reappear now, I was sure: firm, well-appointed and easy to follow. Instead the forest closed inwards, heather snagged my feet and juniper bushes scratched my arms. I walked through dense folds of waterlogged bracken and whippy birch branches that showered me in cloudbursts of miniature rainfall.

Before I realised it the gradient had also began to change. Suddenly I found myself rappelling steeply downhill, clasping at roots and vegetation to slow my momentum. At times I was sliding significant distances, slipping fast through a slick molasses of mud and leaf mulch. I eventually stumbled out from the small section of woodland as if emerging from a jungle. Day-trippers who were making the short walk from Glenmore to the Ryvoan Bothy smiled politely as I shambled past them – my clothes saturated and covered in dark patina of tree-sludge.

It was almost three hours before I reached the mid-point of the Strath Nethy glen. The map's path was still non-existent and I had laboured over ground so soft that my feet disappeared with every step. In one untested stride I had sunk thigh-deep in a cold bog. I panicked briefly, conscious of the solitude of the place, but levered myself out, shaking with adrenalin and the loss of heat.

The valley floor was surprisingly narrow. In places, the distance between the opposing mountains of Cairn Gorm and A'Choinneach was little more than a hundred metres. The Garbh Allt, the small stream that forms the River Nethy, cut a slender course through its centre. It flowed in makeshift movements, spilling around the large blocks of granite that had tumbled hundreds of metres from the crags above.

Some of the boulders were massive. On the other side of the stream, two-thirds of the way up the valley, I noticed a huge section of granite that had come to rest upon several smaller rocks. It formed a large natural shelter and I was sure I had found the elusive refuge mentioned by Henry Alexander:

'In the valley of Garbh Allt, about a mile and a half north of The Saddle, there is a little-known Shelter Stone. It is known locally as Jamie Murray's Cave, and is reputed to have been the hide-out of a well-known poacher in former years. A comfortable bivouac, holding only three with comfort, it lies on the west bank of the Garbh Allt, in a wilderness of other boulders, but it is almost impossible to give precise written directions for finding it.'

From the deepest part of the glen, to look upwards temporarily affected my balance. Dark crenulations of rock formed turrets on the higher slopes and, where the incline permitted, enormous boulders of lateral moraine teetered on precarious outcrops. The El Alamein Refuge was up there somewhere as well, its fastness hidden among the rockfall and glacial debris.

Perhaps it was the extraordinary length of the glen, or maybe its depth, or even a combination of the two, but I began to feel an overwhelming sense of enclosure. Hemmed in by steep hillsides and weighed down by low-pressing clouds I experienced a perceived constriction of space that, for a moment, seemed close to claustrophobia.

Cold, wet and depleted of energy, I started to regret my choice of route through the confines of Strath Nethy's long mountain corridor.

———

It seems only natural that the mountain environment should affect us. Isolation, solitude, topography, terrain and even weather can significantly influence our perception of a place and consequently inform our responses to a particular set of surroundings. Altered sensory stimulation can affect our emotional reasoning and rational processing. In unfamiliar or extreme conditions, feelings can become heightened and abstracted, blurring physical and psychological realities.

I had experienced something similar months earlier as I reached the Oxford's wreckage on Beinn a' Bhuird. Alone on the mist-covered plateau, logical thought had been replaced by irrational feelings. The otherworldliness of the place and the knowledge of its sombre history had changed my perception of the surroundings. Fear and apprehension had quickly taken hold and I had felt a sudden desire to leave the crash-site. It is perhaps this most basic, primal interpretation of an environment that forms the basis of many of the Grey Man occurrences, as well as other unexplained phenomena in the wild.

The reporting of an incorporeal presence has been recorded in many instances of extreme conditions or remoteness worldwide. Perhaps the most famous account of an ethereal companion is from Ernest Shackleton's retelling of his harrowing 'Imperial Trans-Antarctic Expedition' in the epic book, *South*.

Shackleton's third attempt to reach the South Pole was ill-fated from the start. The expedition ship, the

Endurance, became encased within the freezing waters of the Weddell Sea before Shackleton could even commence his expedition on foot. After ten months trapped in the pack-ice, the crew were forced to abandon ship and drag the *Endurance's* small lifeboats across the ice floes for a further five months before they were once again able to set sail in open water.

After reaching land on Elephant Island, Shackleton decided to leave the majority of his crew and continue onwards with five other men to the nearest place of human habitation, a whaling station on the island of South Georgia. Incredibly, the journey was made in a twenty-foot boat across some of the most treacherous seas on the planet and lasted for over fifteen days.

Despite eventually making landfall on South Georgia, safely but severely weakened, their travails were not over. To reach the whaling station on the opposite side of the island required a crossing on foot of its glacier-filled, mountainous interior. It was during this final, exhausting journey that Shackleton and the two men that joined him experienced what has popularly been described since as 'The Third Man Syndrome'. Shackleton and both of his crew members reported afterwards that during their arduous traverse of South Georgia they were assisted by an unseen presence. 'When I look back at those days I have no doubt that Providence guided us, not only across those snow-fields, but across the storm-white sea that separated Elephant Island from our landing-place on South Georgia. I know that during that long and racking march of thirty-six hours over the unnamed mountains and glaciers of South Georgia it seemed to me often that we were four, not three.'

The idea of a benevolent, ethereal companion in times

of extreme duress is present in many other explorative accounts. In his book *The Third Man Factor*, John Geiger recounts many similar cases of a sensed presence, in particular during several epic mountaineering ventures.

So convinced was the English climber Frank Smythe that a fellow climber was descending with him on his 1933 failed attempt on Everest, that he instinctively offered his unseen climbing partner some of his Kendal mint cake; likewise, the legendary climber Reinhold Messner experienced 'The Third Man' during his agonising solo climb of Nanga Parbat, as did the Australian climber, Greg Child, on his thwarted ascent of Broad Peak. In every instance the presence was understood by each climber to be a sustaining and protective force, guiding and strengthening their will in the most desperate of circumstances.

But while most accounts of an unexplained presence are reported as helpful and benign, Geiger also details occasions, most notably amidst the blank expanses of the Polar expeditions, where the presence has been a more sinister, even malevolent manifestation.

Such feelings of intense fear or foreboding have often been associated with anecdotes of the Grey Man. In 1943, during ten days climbing alone in the Cairngorms, the well-known Cairngorm climber, Alexander Tewnion, discharged his service revolver in fright at what he thought was the Grey Man. Tewnion had reached the mist-swathed summit of Ben Macdui when the 'atmosphere became dark and oppressive'. Tewnion reported hearing 'an odd sound [that] echoed through the mist – a loud footstep, it seemed.' He then became convinced that something was approaching him. 'A strange shape loomed up, receded, came charging at me! Without hesitation I whipped out the revolver and fired three times at the figure. When it still came on I turned and hared down the path, reaching Glen Derry in a time that I have never bettered.'

To be alone on or near Ben Macdui it seems, has the potential to provoke feelings of menace that are hard to rationalise. Affleck Grey retells the experience of Richard Frere, a climbing colleague of Peter Densham. Frere was convinced of the veracity of his own terrifying experience on Ben Macdui:

> Tell me that the . . . Presence was only the creation of a mind that was accustomed to take too great an interest in such things. I shall not be convinced. Come, rather, with me at the mysterious dusk time when day and night struggle upon the mountains. Feel the night wind on your faces, and hear it crying amid the rocks. See the desert uplands consumed before racing storms. Though your nerves be of steel, and your mind says it cannot be, you will be acquainted with that fear without a name, that intense dread of the unknown that has pursued mankind from the very dawn of time.

Close to dusk, I eventually found my way out of Strath Nethy. The hours spent walking in the boggy confines of the glen had felt oppressive, at times even dispiriting, but I was pleased to have got through such an enshrouded portal to the range. It made reaching the Saddle, the 800m-high pass into the Loch Avon Basin, feel as though I was accessing a protected gateway, a kind of guarded entry-point into the heart of the Cairngorms.

On the southern side of the Saddle, the land slipped away steeply towards Loch Avon and I remembered

Adam Watson's cautionary words written in the SMC guide to the Cairngorms about entering into the Loch Avon Basin. 'Anyone descending to it…especially in winter, should remember that he is going to one of the most inaccessible places in the Cairngorms, and that to escape he will either have to climb out again or else walk miles down the uninhabited Glen Avon.'

Even in the half-light, the loch resonated with colour. Indented on the shoreline were golden crescents; small half-moon beaches with bleached yellow sands and water gleaming in deepening shades of blue. I tracked the edge of the loch for over two kilometres in the twilight. The open water darkened as I walked and storm clouds scudded high above the cliffs that encircled the basin.

At the head of the glen I could make out the silhouette of the Sticil. Better known as the Shelter Stone Crag, the colossal tooth-shaped cliff face served as a waymark for my destination. At over 250 metres high, the Sticil is so singularly large it is easily the most impressive rock feature in the Cairngorms, if not in Britain. The cliffs are so imposing up close that for 'a climber standing boggle-eyed below its concave prow,' the climber and writer Greg Strange observed, 'the upper rocks appear to tilt over the vertical, an illusion which compounds the impression of impregnability.' Below the crag, somewhere in the scattering of gargantuan rocks, I would find the Shelter Stone cave.

It was late when I reached the wide clearing at the western end of Glen Avon. I was tired and cold from the hard miles that I had covered, and I hoped for company at the shelter. I clambered in darkness among the maze of oversized boulders searching for the cave and its entrance, trying to recall the various descriptions I had read of it.

'The Shelter Stone, or Clach Dhion in Gaelic, is possibly the best known of all the mountain shelters in Scotland,' wrote Ian Thomson. 'It is the largest of the many boulders which lie, scattered over a wide area, at the base of the Shelter Stone Crag from which they tumbled in one or more gigantic rock falls. The enormous Shelter Stone boulder itself came to rest on four smaller boulders, thus forming a roomy chamber underneath, offering sufficient space for seven or so in reasonable comfort, while in an emergency up to thirty could huddle together safe within its confines. The entrance, which faces north-north-east, is narrow and low but this makes for less draught and the shelter has been made fairly wind-tight by packing stones, sods and heather into the chinks in its defences . . . The roof of the howff slopes upwards towards the back so that one can stand almost erect in that part of shelter, a pleasure not permitted nearer to the doorway. A liberal bedding of heather makes for considerable comfort during the long hours of darkness within.'

I had expected to hear voices or be drawn by the glow of torchlight. Instead the cave was unoccupied but simple to find; situated two thirds of the way up the giant rock-fan. The entrance was dark and tucked below what had to be the largest single boulder I have ever seen: a massive, flat-fronted rock the height of a house. I had to remove my rucksack and stoop low to get in. I scanned the interior with my head-torch, staying low for fear of banging my head. The air inside was cold and my breath steamed in the thin cone of torch light.

The narrow entranceway opened up into a surprisingly large space within. Further, darker recesses and chambers were visible at the back of the cave. The beam of my torch picked out various random objects: a collapsible camping stool; burnt-out candles; old sleeping mats; a lighter and the inevitable odd sock. Despite the rain, the place was completely dry. At the back of the shelter I was able to stand almost fully upright and I laid out my sleeping bag and quickly piled on all the clothes I had with me.

It felt strange to be settling down for the night with a boulder of such immense weight directly above me. The eminent Cairngorm mountaineer, A. I. McConnochie, had once measured the Shelter Stone's dimensions and approximated its weight to be 1,700 tonnes. A later calculation made in 1926, based on a sample of the Shelter Stone, however, revised the estimate down to a mere 1,361 tonnes.

To sleep in such a cave requires a psychological readjustment, a putting of trust in the shelter's structural integrity. In *Mountain Days and Bothy Nights* Dave Brown and Ian Mitchell retell a story of a cave-dwelling loss of nerve under another famous Scottish boulder.

Five young Glaswegian climbers had packed themselves into the space under one of the Narnain Boulders, high up on the slopes of the Cobbler in the Arrochar Alps. Room was tight, so the smallest of the group had to squeeze himself into a claustrophobic recess at the back of the cave. 'Everything was peaceful enough until the small hours when everyone was wrenched from sleep by a cry from deep within the recess. "*The boulder's falling! The boulder's falling!*" ' The climbers immediately raised their hands against the roof of the cave, then, 'realising that they must have looked very peculiar lying on their backs straining to stop, with their bare hands, a multi-ton piece of rock from falling on them, they simultaneously burst into laughter that was both hysterical and relieved.'

I felt reassured though, by knowing the history of the shelter, for it has been in use for centuries. It was described as far back as 1794 in the *Statistical Account* as a place of sanctuary for 'freebooters', with enough space to shelter eighteen armed men. During the Second World War, the Shelter Stone was used frequently by large Commando parties training in the range, and the British Prime Minister, Ramsay MacDonald, had also once spent a night in the cave, as have a whole host of climbing luminaries over the years.

More than once, however, the cave has also been associated with misfortune. On 9 June 1930, a student from London, who had stayed the night in the Shelter Stone, died the next day after collapsing from fatigue on Ben Macdui. Tragically, in the case of Alistair Mackenzie and Duncan Ferrier who perished in a storm on Cairn Gorm three years later, in January 1933, it was their decision to leave the safety of the Shelter Stone and attempt to reach home through fierce blizzard conditions that ultimately cost them their lives.

Few other places in Britain, in fact, can claim to have such a rich mountaineering heritage. It was here at the Shelter Stone that the oldest surviving climbing club in Scotland was formed in 1887. The Cairngorm Club came into existence the day after Queen Victoria's Golden Jubilee. Six hillwalking enthusiasts from Aberdeen who had gathered to commemorate the occasion by releasing fireworks from the summit of Ben Macdui, 'spontaneously and unanimously agreed', the following day, by the banks of Loch Avon 'to form the Cairngorm Club', resolving to open their ranks 'to the admission of men and women of heroic spirit, and possessed of souls open to the influences of nature pure and simple as displayed among our loftiest mountains.'

Sleep was difficult in the cave. A draught flowed continuously from the entranceway and I struggled in vain to get warm. Depleted of energy, and cold and wet from the long walk in, I lay shuddering within my sleeping bag. I managed only a light slumber; awoken intermittently throughout the night by the cold and by the scuttling of rodents. At one point, I came to at the sound of rockfall outside. The noise was terrific. A thunderous metallic report, followed briefly by silence, then milliseconds later, an even louder crack as the rock ricocheted down the hillside past me.

At dawn, a gas-blue light filled the cave and I was able to make out the interior of the chamber: the smooth granite underside of the giant boulder above me and the pinpricks of daylight showing through gaps in the shelter's makeshift walls. I ached from my night's rest: the hard floor and the constant shivering had left my muscles stiff and painful, but I felt elated by the experience. I had slept in a cave! It seemed an inherently wilder way to have stayed outdoors than to have simply pitched camp.

It was also thrilling to have stayed somewhere of such antiquity. It is impossible to know exactly how long the Shelter Stone has been in its current position; centuries certainly, possibly millennia, perhaps even predating the Neolithic. I doubted that I could have slept anywhere with a more historic series of inhabitants.

Near the entranceway I flicked through the pages of the visitors book, reading about some of the shelter's more recent guests: a mix of climbers and hillwalkers mainly, attempting routes on some of the big walls nearby or simply passing through. Outside, morning was beginning to filter into the glen. I sat on some nearby rocks, my legs drawn up to my chest to keep warm, and ate breakfast. The storms of the preceding days had passed and I watched coppery clouds skim slowly above the surrounding peaks. The proportions of the Loch Avon Basin were, at first, hard to register. 'Nothing could be grander or wilder,' wrote Queen Victoria when she had visited in 1861. It was true; the place felt wild on an almost prehistoric scale: sheer slopes, hundreds of feet deep, plunged into the glen with cataracts spilling from the surface of the plateau.

The artists George Fennel Robson, Edwin Landseer and August Becker all painted Loch Avon during the nineteenth century. Each of the paintings of the glen are similar in the way they depict it. They are subjective interpretations, deliberately ignoring the constraints of accuracy. Each is imbued with the characteristic exaggerations of Sublime landscape art: the overstated mountains, the disproportionately large cliffs and glowering skies. Yet Loch Avon seems to lend itself easily to such embellishments.

It is a massively inverted landscape, a geological imprint, glacially carved and still crumbling in on itself. It is an area, as well, that is capable of violent and rapid transformation. In August 1964, Eric Langmuir, the Principal of Glenmore Lodge and author of the iconic mountaineering manual *Mountaincraft and Leadership*, witnessed 'the most amazing natural phenomenon' he had ever seen near the Shelter Stone Crag.

Langmuir had descended into Loch Avon with a group of friends including the climber, Jock Nimlin. The weather was warm and clear, but in the distance Langmuir happened to notice 'great towering cumulus clouds over Ben Macdui and beyond'. The walk was uneventful until the party crossed the small bridge over the Feith Buidhe stream.

Suddenly Langmuir spotted a large bird hovering above the Shelter Stone Crag. Believing it to be an eagle, he shouted to his companions, only moments later to realise 'it was not an eagle at all, but a huge boulder which seemed to be airborne', and the first 'of an incredible bombardment of stones which was to last a full half-hour'. Langmuir, his wife and their companions looked on 'mesmerised' as the incredible geomorphic event unfolded.

> We could hear a sort of roaring noise . . . we saw that all the screes on the Shelter Stone side of Loch Avon were starting to move . . . any larger rock that happened to be lying on the surface was immediately sent tumbling down. So, on the back of all these screes was a torrent of boulders plunging down the hillside.

Enthralled and aghast at what they were witnessing, the group failed to notice the change in Feith Buidhe. Within thirty minutes the small stream had risen by over two feet, completely covering the footbridge they had just crossed. Realising the gravity of the situation, the proximity of the landslides and the intensity of the flash floods, Langmuir and his friends rushed to leave the scene. 'We grabbed our bags and made a dash for the bridge, and just at that point all the screes on the other side – that is the Cairn Gorm side – of the Feith Buidhe started to crash down.'

By this point the circumstances seemed grave. 'There we were in the middle of the corrie with screes ploughing down all around us – and boulders plunging down the screes.' Despite his extensive mountaineering experience, Langmuir wondered if they were doing the right thing, 'because, as we crossed the bridge and ran down the footpath on the Cairn Gorm side, some boulders were crossing the path and crashing into Loch Avon.'

The incident seemed so perilous to Langmuir that he issued desperate instructions. 'I was really concerned that we might get trapped between a number of these screes. It would have been very difficult to dodge a salvo of these enormous rocks. I shouted to my wife to jump into the loch if it looked as though we were going to get hit.'

Luckily the group survived unscathed, escaping with their lives what Langmuir later described as 'one of the most remarkable experiences of my mountaineering life.'

Such is the verticality of the Basin that climbers have been drawn here for decades. The earliest forays were made on the Sticil and Carn Etchachan with Henry Raeburn and a handful of others claiming a smattering of first ascents in the early twentieth century. Remarkably, the area then remained unchallenged for decades. It was not until the 1950s that it once again attracted significant climbing attention. A prolific band of Aberdeen climbers, including the irrepressible Tom Patey, posted numerous new routes on the large rock-walls of the Shelter Stone Crag, Hell's Lum Crag and Stag Rocks, that by the early 1970s set the scene for an historic winter climb.

January 1970 marked a watershed moment in British climbing. Up until that point, techniques for winter mountaineering had remained largely undeveloped since the early Alpinists took to Britain's mountains in the nineteenth century. The ascent of steep snow or ice-covered slopes required the cutting of steps and hand-holds. Divots were hewed out of the ice with the adze of an axe to provide small ledges to support upward movement. The procedure was time-consuming, physically draining and technically difficult.

'In really tough snow or snow-ice steps are difficult to cut and many blows may be required,' wrote J. E. Q. Barford in 1946, in the Pelican Books guide to *Climbing in Britain*. 'The step should always be made so as to slope slightly inwards,' Barford instructed. 'In cutting steps you should stand upright, in balance, grip the shaft with both hands if you can, swing it no higher than your head, preserve rhythm in your strokes and, as far as possible, let the weight of the axe do the work.'

The method was also, by its nature, limited in application. Steeper ice walls were impossible to scale by merely cutting steps, leaving many routes unclimbable in winter. While the standard ten-pointed crampons and traditional longer ice axes provided climbers with a degree of purchase on compacted slopes, their effectiveness diminished as the incline increased towards the vertical. To be able to conquer many of Scotland's winter crags a quantum leap in climbing techniques was required.

That moment came on a single climb on Hell's Lum Crag in the Loch Avon Basin. Wearing twelve-pointed crampons with two front-projecting points and holding 'ice daggers' in each hand, the maverick Glasgow climber John Cunningham successfully managed to pick his way up 'The Chancer': at the time, the steepest single pitch of ice that had ever been climbed in Scotland.

The technique was not completely new. Austrian and German climbers had been using front-pointing crampons for some time. Cunningham had also previously experimented with their use during his time spent with the British Antarctic Survey, where he had discovered that by kicking the sharp front points into the ice-wall of a nearby glacier he was able to stand upright at an angle of 80 degrees without support for his hands. When this technique was combined with hammering in ice daggers for handholds, Cunningham was convinced that vertical ice could be ascended.

The Loch Avon Basin and, in particular, Hell's Lum Crag, were ideal places for Cunningham to test his new technique. Climbing the large icefall of the The Chancer, which 'seemed to impend like the side of a huge barrel', would have been unthinkable with traditional step-cutting, but Cunningham's futuristic approach succeeded. From that point on the blueprint for winter climbing was to change. Cunningham's bold innovations on the ice-plastered rock-walls of Loch Avon shifted the boundaries of the possible, forever redefining climbers' battle with verticality.

⬛

From a distance, Britain's second-highest mountain is often invisible. It is cloistered safely away from sight, hidden deeply within the landmass of the Cairngorm plateau. Up close, Ben Macdui's profile is often equally hard to detect, its boundaries uncertain and its shape morphed into the high ground that surrounds it. It is a geography of unexpected secrecy and concealment, a seemingly counter-intuitive proposition: landscape possessing both altitude and anonymity.

It is perhaps the topography of Ben Macdui, however, that gives rise to its mysteries. In snow or cloud cover, its summit ridges are vast and homogenous. If approached from the north, as it most frequently is, the terrain can appear monotonous and repetitive, an environment where sensory stimulation can be reduced to an absolute minimum.

In the visual and aural blankness that can occur on Ben Macdui, thought processes can become altered, drawn towards the imaginary and hallucinatory. Like the many instances of spectral companions which have been recorded by the explorers of other featureless places, aviators, astronauts and deep-sea divers, it is possible that the Big Grey Man may simply be a neuronal projection, the mind's attempt to populate the mountain's unfamiliar empty spaces.

Mountains, though, can also be an arena for powerful natural forces, phenomena unobserved at lower elevations. Climbers in the world's higher ranges are often witness to strange experiences arising from combinations of climate and height: the foreboding hum of metallic climbing gear in the moments before an electrical storm; the hypoxic delusions born of oxygen-thin air or the intensely dry and ionized Föhn winds, which are said to provoke episodes of madness.

Ghosts have also frequently been reported on mountains. Apparitions in warped human form appear, enormous shadow figures with elongated limbs whose distorted movements mimic those of their petrified viewers. Occasionally these sightings can appear in news stories. The observers are simply unable to explain their terrifying experiences, but adamant that they occurred.

The cause, however, is simple: it is the result of sunlight casting the shape of an individual onto a bank of cloud, magnifying their outline against the blank canvas of mist. A diffraction of light also ensues, surrounding the spectral image with a peculiar halo of rainbow light.

The phenomenon is known as the 'Brocken Spectre'. Like the tricks of the mind that can fill the sensory void of wild places, the Brocken Spectre is a projection, a fleeting *trompe l'oeil* seen only by the individual whose shape is rendered upon the clouds. It is an effect, therefore, that is also entirely personal in its communication and expression.

I thought of the places a Brocken Spectre would be likely to appear on Ben Macdui. They would be locations favouring a screening of cloud and strong directional light. There were the east-facing cliffs above Lochan Uaine, or Lurcher's Crag where mist can billow upwards from the Lairig Ghru, or anywhere on the steep western flank of the mountain.

It is possible that the combination of Ben Macdui's topography and climate are somehow predisposed to the generation of ghostly sightings. In its height and rounded, plateaued form, Ben Macdui resonates closely with the eponymous mountain where the Brocken Spectre was first recorded. Like Ben Macdui, the Brocken peak, in the Harz region of northern Germany, is a large tableland of curving, whale-back granite, prone to substantial mist and rainfall. Like Ben Macdui, the Brocken is also a peak steeped in myth and supernatural significance. It is a place with long-standing associations to paganism and ancient religions and is referenced in Goethe's play *Faust*, as the rendezvous where 'the witches ride' to congregate on Walpurgis Night.

Such cultural recognition also exists for Ben Macdui. A peak ubiquitously known for its anecdotal rather than visual identity, it is a mountain effectively defined by its own narrative.

For once, I had hoped for poor weather, low cloud and cloying mist, to create the atmosphere of the Grey Man sightings. The morning, though, was still and bright. I clambered through the narrow path that led south, out of the Basin, surfacing into sunlight by the shores of another, even higher loch.

At over 900 metres, Loch Etchachan is the largest body of water at this height in Scotland. Such is the altitude of the loch and its sheltered position within the hollow juncture of three mountains, that it remains frozen for well over half a year. I had arrived at the midpoint in its thaw cycle; just a few months since the last of its ice had melted away, but only a dozen or so weeks before the waters would begin to set hard once again.

To reach Ben Macdui's summit I continued south, crossing a small outflow stream and moving upwards on a gradual south-westerly ridge. After twenty minutes I was high above the loch in warm sunshine and able to see other walkers below me – three figures pacing determinedly in single file, and two more dotted further downhill, their long shadows bouncing ahead of them. The gradient eventually lessened and the land began to converge towards the summit. By this stage I was no longer alone. I could see others nearby, approaching from different directions, each moving towards the mountain's triangulation point.

That morning it was hard to believe in the Grey Man stories, and the cold, isolating terror that has apparently gripped so many on Ben Macdui. The sun was already high, rising on its arc, wisps of white cirrus clouds drifted against the blue and a small crowd had gathered at the summit, chatting and laughing together.

The Cat's Den

'To all those whose thoughts are in the wild, untrodden places.'

Seton Gordon, *Afoot in Wild Places.*

I arrived in Rothiemurchus Forest during an Indian winter. For two weeks from the middle of March high pressure systems had dominated Northern Europe, bringing clear nights and plummeting temperatures. Snow had fallen across the country, closing roads and opening ski-runs. I had driven north in Alpine conditions: low evening sun pinking the mountain tops and walls of hard-packed snow, the texture of polystyrene, piled high on the hard shoulder.

In the Cairngorms the snow had been abundant and long-lasting. Avalanches had occurred on many of the leeward slopes and several mountaineers had been killed. Winter had returned, rancorous and full-blown.

I had wanted to make a traverse of the range, moving north to south over the Lairig an Laoigh pass, hoping for glimpses of eagles and snow buntings. But the prospect of venturing alone into the mountains in such unexpected and unpredictable conditions seemed daunting, even foolhardy. Instead, I decided to stay on the peripheries, avoiding the harsh extremes of the plateau and exploring the spaces that I had so often walked through while speeding my way to higher ground. In particular, I wanted to lose myself in the ancient forestry of the range: to wander the remnants of Scotland's once mighty Forest of Caledon.

The arboreal fragments that surround the Cairngorms are unique, for they are viewfinders to the past, a spyhole into a prehistoric landscape: woodland that has existed continuously since the glaciers retreated after the last ice age. Little has changed in these forests for over 6,000 years, but their extent has withered. They have shrunk from a once vast pinewood covering much of northern Scotland to tiny woodland archipelagos: island clusters of mainly pine and birch scattered in isolation across the Highlands.

My journeys in the Cairngorms had often crossed paths with these trees. There were the bone-like fragments of pine I had seen submerged beneath the peat hags of Glen Dee, the forest hideaways of Glen Feshie and my search for capercaillie in the woodland of Glen Quoich. Each interaction, however, had been fleeting and coincidental; brief interludes on the passage to somewhere else.

Now, though, I wanted to understand more about such an endangered and primordial habitat. By deliberately spending time within the forestry I hoped to become temporarily absorbed in its rhythms and occurrences. To be immersed, as the writer Roger Deakin had put it, as if walking 'on something very like the seabed, looking up at a canopy of leaves as if it were the surface of the water, filtering the descending shafts of sunlight and dappling everything.' In doing so, I hoped there would be the chance to see wildlife of exceptional rarity, but exclusive locality: pine martens, crossbills, crested tits, capercaillie and, most elusively, wildcats.

There was also another reason that I wanted to explore Rothiemurchus. For it is a place richly embroidered with history and folklore. Human life has existed in the forest for millennia, imprinting layers of usage and habitation upon the woodland. Traces of the past, both physical and mythological, stratify the ancient pines like the fold lines on an old map.

In particular, there was one story which seemed to straddle the boundaries between fable and reality. It was an apocryphal tale told about a local fugitive, a wanted man who had reputedly evaded capture by hiding in a cave concealed somewhere in the vast expanse of the forest. The whereabouts of the secret hideout (if it existed) were unclear. I could find only vague written references to its location, but I had heard the cave's name mentioned several times; the place was known locally (almost mythically it seemed) as the Cat's Den. It seemed the perfect secret history to search for in the wild forest: a place of feral retreat.

My breath gathered in small, lingering clouds of fog as I sat, huddled on a tree stump. My toes and fingers had begun to go numb and I vibrated with a deep, subcutaneous shiver. I hunched deeper inside my sleeping bag and wrapped the hood of my bivouac bag tight around my head. Above me I watched the celestial spin, charting the movements of constellations, pin-sharp, in the clear sky.

During the previous night the temperature had dropped to minus ten. I had planned to stay out in the forest until morning, in the hope of spotting nocturnal wildlife. But the cold was penetrating to my core. It was becoming impossible to stay warm and I wondered how long I could last before I retreated to my tent.

Several years earlier I had come to the same spot: a small clearing less than a kilometre's walk into the forest from the main road. I was with my three-year-old daughter. We had crept into the trees at dusk. Dark unidentifiable birds darted between the branches and wind moved the canopy. Above us we heard the wheezy cooing of woodpigeons and the clatter of their wing-beats as they moved between their roosts. I felt my daughter's hand squeeze my fingers tighter as we moved further into the forest.

After twenty minutes we stopped, finding a place to sit on a tangle of soft heather, our backs pressed against the girth of scaly pine. As we nestled together in silence, the forest around us began to stir. We heard the rustle of undergrowth nearby and my daughter pushed herself closer into my side. I put my arm around her shoulders and pulled her in tight. We waited for signs of movement in the half-light. I scanned the branches and foliage with my binoculars, hoping for a glimpse of a pine marten or even a wildcat. But there was nothing.

Then suddenly, in the distance, my eye caught rapid motion. Something was moving fast through the trees. A large red deer was hurtling through the forest in blind panic. It was followed seconds later by more deer, fifteen or twenty in total, all running at incredible speed. I watched the blur of animals in amazement. Through the binocular lenses, the column of deer moved noiselessly, cutting their frenetic dash through the trees as if watched on a silent film reel. Within seconds they were gone and my heart was left pounding, my chest rising in short breaths.

Since that night, Rothiemurchus seemed to me a forest that could conjure up unexpected wildness and primitiveness. It was the kind of place to experience the same kind of 'glorious surprises' that Desmond Nethersole-

Thompson and Adam Watson referred to when chancing upon the elusive wildlife of the Cairngorms. 'You may suddenly come upon a fox or wildcat sound asleep in long heather, or a couple of foxes frisking like puppies along a bare ridge,' wrote Nethersole-Thompson and Watson in lyrical terms. 'A shrew suddenly runs at your feet, moving like a clockwork mouse over the snow. In the winter sun a pure white ermine stoat shines like a light against a dark peat bank. You watch a squirrel's bushy red tail swirling as it leaps from branch to branch in the depths of a green pine. Or you see a fox, looking jet black as it crosses the snowy tops in the blinding April sun. In the blizzard you gaze at a white hare, its ears low and its back to the wind, squatting snugly behind a ridge.'

Such encounters, though, are uncommon. The mammals that inhabit the range are shy and reclusive, often with crepuscular lives, hunting, feeding and moving in the hours of dusk and dawn, or sometimes exclusively at night. To come across Cairngorm's secretive wildlife often requires deliberate planning or coincides with ventures at the edges of day: the early-morning start to a walk or the dusk-filled return through the forest.

Pine martens, in particular, are adapted to an almost entirely nocturnal existence. Few people, therefore, are ever lucky enough to see one in the wild. The animal's preference for night-time activity precludes easy sightings during the day, but their present-day elusiveness is also attributable to the effects of human repression.

During the nineteenth century the pine marten experienced an almost catastrophic population decline in Britain. So much so, that by the early twentieth century, habitat destruction, persecution and trapping for its valuable fur had reduced the pine marten's once extensive

distributional range across Britain to mere relict populations. The pine marten was forced to live out a near fugitive
existence, retreating to mountainous regions of moorland
and forestry, predominately in isolated areas of north-west
Scotland. It was in these Highland strongholds, however,
that the pine marten was able to survive and expand. During the twentieth century, increases in commercial forest
plantations, a reduction in the number of gamekeepers
and culling and eventually, full legal protection for the
species in 1988, has meant that pine martens have now
recolonised several other regions of Scotland.

Rothiemurchus and the other forest areas surrounding the Cairngorm range provide superb habitats for pine
martens, for the species has evolved as a woodland specialist: expert climbers and hunters, as adept at chasing
prey through the tree-tops as they are at hunting on the
forest floor. Martens prefer mature coniferous cover, making dens in hollow trees, squirrel dreys and even birds'
nests. The forest also provides much of their diverse diet:
a ready supply of wood mice, voles, rabbits, hares, birds,
insects and even berries and fungi.

I had never seen a pine marten, but I had often looked
for the tell-tale signs of their presence: well-worn runs
imprinted on the forest floor, scats deposited on prominent rocks to mark their territories or sounds indicating
that they were the focus of defensive mobbing by birds.
There would, of course, be no mistaking the sighting of
a pine marten. Like other members of the weasel family, their bodies are long and slender but their fur is a
darker brown than that of stoats or weasels and their tail
is visibly bushier. Their buttery-orange throat patch, large
rounded ears and heart-shaped face also set them apart
conclusively from other British mustelids.

Between 1880 and 1890 pine martens actually became extinct in the Avon and Spey valleys. Now, though, the forests of Rothiemurchus, Glenmore and Abernethy support significant populations. Bolder individuals have even been known to frequent local gardens, tempted to bird tables, showing a particular preference for jam sandwiches and peanut butter.

I was becoming seriously cold. The night air had the same ambient chill as an industrial deep-freeze, and my lungs rasped with each intake of breath. I wriggled my toes in my boots and stuffed my hands tight under my armpits, but I still couldn't get warm. The moon was low in the sky, large and lantern-yellow, silhouetting a fretwork of bare branches. The moonlight threw long shadows on the forest floor, casting the trunks of pines horizontally like fallen trees and illuminating the undergrowth in binary relief: silver and black.

I had heard noises: the mirror calls of owls, and, at one point, an unnerving, indeterminate disturbance from somewhere deeper in the forest. But despite the sharp clarity of the night, I had not seen anything. Desperate to get warm, I eventually returned to my tent, feeling strangely self-conscious as I trod quietly among the dark trees.

'It would be difficult,' reflected the naturalist William MacGillivray, referring to the higher peaks of the Cairngorms, 'for a person not looking at these mountains, to imagine the beauty which they have so suddenly received . . . How beautifully their white summits contrast with the blue sky above, and the purple hue of the lower hills, or the dark green of the solemn Pine-forests.'

MacGillivray's book, *The Natural History of Dee Side and Braemar* is one of the earliest and most extensive written accounts of the Cairngorms. It is a work fascinating not merely as a record of the natural history at the time, but also for the literary precedent it sets.

The first reading is deceptive. The impression given is of a scientifically rigorous field-guide, detailed and analytical, primarily concerned, it would appear, with record-keeping and observation; a diligent cataloguing of species, geology and habitats.

Yet closer reading reveals something else. Sentimentality and astonishment permeate the text. At times MacGillivray struggles to contain his wonderment at his surroundings, defaulting to more exultant tones.

> All around, mountains appeared behind mountains . . . The beams of the setting sun darted here and there through the clouds, which exhibited a hundred ever-varying shades. In one direction, a vast livid mass hung over the ridges of a mountain, its lower fringed margin beautifully tinged with deep crimson. In another place, the white vapour which clung to the summits of the mountains, assumed, where opposed to the sunbeam, a roseate hue of the greatest delicacy.

The scientific disciplines of objectivity and empiricism are frequently discarded in MacGillivray's writing, as he veers towards an almost maudlin interest in the wildlife and landscape of the Cairngorms. 'Shall I rejoice or take up a lamentation?' he wrote, trying to rationalise his emotional response to a particular Cairngorm view. 'Subjects of gladness and grief are before me.'

The Natural History of Dee Side is an important but

overlooked work in the lineage of British nature writing. A successor to the naturalist Gilbert White and a contemporary of John Clare, MacGillivray's scientific immersion in and stocktaking of the natural history of the Cairngorms modulate into unabashed lyrical descriptions. It is an irrepressible mingling of rational enquiry and romantic appreciation, poetry surfacing amid the cold exactitudes of scientific language.

Written before the publication of Thoreau's vastly more celebrated *Walden* and almost half a century before the writings of John Muir, *The Natural History of Dee Side* foreshadows similar notions of connectivity with nature and wild places. MacGillivray's writing and his solitary wanderings in the Cairngorm landscape make a philosophical statement. He asserts a parallel claim to the kind of individualism and self-reliance espoused in the doctrines of American Transcendentalism and the writing that followed.

MacGillivray also set an exploratory example for the Cairngorms and beyond. To truly study natural history, MacGillivray believed, was to intimately observe the natural environment at close quarters. In short, MacGillivray understood that the naturalist must 'put himself in danger, and subject himself to fatigues and hardships.' This was a view that was stridently at odds with the cabinet-naturalists of the era, who preferred instead to concern themselves with the minutiae of taxonomy and classification, often far removed from the hard realities of fieldwork. MacGillivray had little time for the petty squabbles of the cabinet-naturalists and a mutual antipathy existed with many of his wealthy, scientific peers. 'I am tired of the dull reality of common life,' MacGillivray declared, in stark contrast to the comfortable cameraderie of scientific societies, professing instead to be 'passionately fond of adventures.'

MacGillivray's commitment to life as a field naturalist was whole-hearted, and as a result he became a prodigious walker. At the age of 23 he decided to visit the British Museum in London, walking a circuitous route from his home in Aberdeen, covering a remarkable distance of 828 miles in just eight weeks, an average of almost 15 miles every day.

MacGillivray's inclination for explorations on foot and his astonishing stamina served him well in the Cairngorms. In writing *The Natural History of Dee Side* he ranged a vast geographic area of inhospitable and largely uncharted terrain. My favourite passage of the book captures something of MacGillivray's doughty resilience and physical fortitude. The description is of a trip in the upper reaches of what must be Garbh Coire. MacGillivray is alone, miles from the nearest dwelling and sleeping rough with only the most basic equipment.

About midnight I looked up and saw the moon, with some stars. They were at times obscured by masses of vapour, which rolled along the summits of the mountains . . . I was near the upper end of a high valley, completely surrounded by masses of rock . . . on awakening from my slumber, I felt chilly, and soon after began to shiver. I then rose, and gathered a few large stones, and a good deal of grass and long heath, with which I formed a somewhat snug couch. Then, eating a little of my scanty store of barley bread, and drinking two or three cupfuls of water from a neighbouring rill, I lay down, put heather and my knapsack over my feet, placed myself in an easy posture and fell asleep.

Despite the significance of *The Natural History of Dee Side*, the book was lucky to ever get published, and MacGillivray never saw the printed version in his lifetime. The manuscript was eventually bought by Queen Victoria who, inspired by all things pertaining to Deeside, published the book by royal command for 'private circulation', several years after the author's death in 1855. MacGillivray's most accessible work, however, like his legacy, remains sadly under-acknowledged. His caustic, highly-sensitised and fiery temperament did little to endear him to his peers, and his scientific achievements at the time, and since, have never fully been recognised.

Yet MacGillivray is one of Britain's most important naturalists. He was a supremely talented man: academically gifted and robustly fit, he was also a brilliant wildlife artist. He collaborated with the famous American ornithological illustrator, J. J. Audubon, and produced a prolific output of beautifully detailed watercolours, now housed in the Natural History Museum. He is also credited with almost single-handedly establishing the foundations for modern ornithology, and through his appointment as Regius Professor of Natural History at the University of Aberdeen, he revolutionised the way in which natural history was taught, emphasising the importance of observational fieldwork.

His research for *The Natural History of Dee Side* however, took its toll. The distances covered and conditions endured, particularly in the Cairngorms, would have been difficult for anyone at the time. For MacGillivray, then in his fifties, the effort and privations eventually became too much. He fell ill and died in 1852, but not before completing his seminal contribution to the literature of the Cairngorms. A book, though barely appreciated at the time, that set the template for a succession of Cairngorm naturalists.

—

By morning, frost had formed. A dusty-white crust layered the surface of the forest. Leaves, branches and undergrowth were platinum-plated, crystalline and sparkling. The sun had already risen and cut diagonal shafts into the forest floor. Where the sunbeams fell, they warmed and backlit the ice so that the heather gleamed with thousands of glittering dewdrops, each capturing tiny prisms of rainbow sunlight.

The sunshine and blue sky were deceptive. It was still desperately cold. My water-bottle was thick with ice. It sloshed inside in mushy floes that blocked the spout when I tried to drink from it. I wanted to get warm, so I began walking, heading roughly south with no particular course. My intention, by way of wandering, was eventually to reach one of the most celebrated areas of Rothiemurchus: the two tree-fringed lochs in the middle of the forest.

Loch an Eilein and its smaller feeder loch, Loch Gamhna, are Rothiemurchus's showpiece visitor attraction. For centuries the lochs have been venerated as an area of outstanding natural beauty and have been frequented by tourists avidly since the nineteenth century. In 1907, the writer Hugh Macmillan was so spellbound by the lochs' setting, he wrote about it in rapturous tones. 'Its beauty touches some of the deepest chords of the heart. It is not a mere landscape, it is an altar piece.'

In the same year, A. I. McConnochie, in his *Guide to Aviemore and Vicinity* described it as 'one of the most beautiful spots in Scotland'. 'Certainly nothing can equal it in Speyside,' McConnochie commented. So much so, that 'in summer it is visited by all manner of conveyances, from Kingussie on the one hand and Grantown on the other, not to mention hundreds who over the course of the season make a special journey from much greater distances.'

It was here, though, amid the postcard scenery of Rothiemurchus's forested lochs that I hoped to find the Cat's Den. In one of the few written references I had found about the cave, McConnochie describes its rough location, as being in the crags somewhere above Loch Gamhna. 'The Cat's Den,' McConnochie wrote, 'is on Creagan à Chait of Kennapole Hill, and is a curious recess in the rock.'

Just like Nan Shepherd, who described the 'deep narrow chasm among the Kennapol [sic] rocks' as one of the 'hiding-holes of hunted men', McConnochie also knew of the 'legendary history' of the Cat's Den.

The cave, so the story goes, was once the hideout of Sandy Grant, also known as 'Black Sandy' – a servant of the local laird. Black Sandy's infamy and his status as a fugitive were assured after a particularly brutal incident involving a housekeeper at one of the laird's residences.

Legend has it that the laird's son had become besotted with the housekeeper and that they had several illegitimate children together. Concerned that his estate would eventually fall into the hands of the housekeeper and her children, the laird summoned the assistance of Black Sandy to end the relationship. Black Sandy's approach to the task was simple and vicious. In an attempt to end the interest of the laird's son in the housekeeper, he decided to disfigure her by cutting off her ears. Local people were outraged by the incident, and though he had taken the precaution of disguising himself during the attack, Black Sandy fled the forest for fear of reprisals. He moved briefly to Grantown, but once again found reason to go into hiding. During an argument with a drover he almost killed the man, leaving him for dead near the Spey Bridge, and returned in secret to Rothiemurchus where he concealed himself in the Cat's Den.

Black Sandy was never captured. It is rumoured that he made his escape to America, where he found freedom and financial success and was, if the legend is to be believed, an ancestor of President Ulysses Grant.

For most of the morning I roamed the forest aimlessly, stravaiging among the trees. Where I could, I followed the non-human tracks: the faint, habit-trails of woodland animals. The routes were etched by deer, I guessed, or badgers, which had pressed lines of continual passage into the forest floor. Mostly, though, I moved through the thick briar of heather and blaeberry, edging between threadbare juniper branches that would hold clusters of blue-grey berries the colour of smoke.

I stopped frequently, trying inexpertly to blend in with my surroundings. At one point, as I sat and ate breakfast, I saw three species of birds all at the same time. Each moved with a simultaneous but unsynchronised action: the blow-pipe darts of blue-tits, the stitchwork rise and fall of a woodpecker and the corkscrew climb of a treecreeper.

It was hard to really escape human influences in the forest. My own meandering route crossed several of the man-made paths that transect Rothiemurchus. Some of the tracks are ancient in their origins, rights of way used for centuries for droving cattle, or in the case of the Thieves Road, for stealing it. There was also the 'Loggers

Route', a path recently reconditioned for use as a cycle track, but which owes its existence to the industry that it once served.

Tree-felling altered the complexion of the forest more than any other human activity. At various points in Rothiemurchus's history vast areas of its trees have been cleared. The first significant, large-scale exploitation of timber resources came after the Jacobite Rebellion in 1715. Several large forfeited estates were sold to speculators from the south and commercial deforestation continued in earnest until around 1850, when iron instead of wood became used more readily in shipbuilding. Industrial logging activities resumed during the First World War when members of the specialist Canadian Forest Corps were enlisted to carry out the work.

Quite apart from the actual loss of trees, the industry changed the forest in other ways. Sawmills were created and the tributaries of the Spey – the Luinneag, the Milton Burn and Beannaidh, were adapted for floating logs downstream by the construction of artificial embankments and sluice-gates, the evidence of which can still be seen in the forest today. 'It was a busy scene all through the forest,' wrote the diarist Elizabeth Grant in *Memoirs of a Highland Lady*, 'small sawmills had been erected wherever there was sufficient water-power, near part of the forest where felling was going on . . . It was picturesque to come suddenly out of the gloom of the pine-trees, on to a little patch of cultivation near a stream with a cottage or two, and a saw-mill at work'.

Despite Grant's bucolic description, life for the loggers was hard. The work was gruelling and dangerous, with poor living conditions. The plight of the floaters – the men responsible for moving the logs downstream – was particularly wretched. The employment was seasonal and often necessitated staying in temporary lodgings while the work took place. Grant describes one such form of accommodation in miserable detail.

> A large bothy was built for them at the mouth of the Druie in a fashion that suited themselves; a fire on a stone hearth in the middle of the floor, a hole in the very centre of the roof just over it where some of the smoke got out, heather spread on the ground, no window, and there after their hard day's work, they lay down for the night in their wet clothes – for they had been perhaps hours in the river – each man's feet to the fire, each man's plaid round his chest, a circle of wearied bodies half-stupefied by whiskey, enveloped in a cloud of steam and smoke.

For a while I followed one of the forest's main paths, heading north towards Gleann Einich. Just right of the path in a little clearing, I passed a small building, a woodlander's dwelling. The cottage was low and rectangular, whitewashed with small, curtainless windows which were set directly below a roof made from corrugated iron that was painted bright terracotta red. There were chimneys at each of the gable ends – a hearth for each of the main rooms. A caravan had been set outside the cottage, its original white finish dulled by years of mould and tree-dust. Next to the caravan was an old bath, and beyond that, at the far side of the cottage, was a woodshed, leaning at an angle, piled with timber covered in a blue tarpaulin. The place felt half-abandoned, as if only recently deserted. It was reminiscent of other similar uninhabited buildings that I knew of nearby, some in more advanced states of disrepair: former farmsteads, that like the sawmills and the loggers' bothies which once occupied Rothiemurchus, had been left to disintegrate, being slowly reclaimed by the forest.

—

In Britain, the veneration of wildlife is a newly acquired sentiment, an appreciation of relatively contemporary origins. As recently as the turn of the twentieth century an interest in British wildlife existed mainly as an interest in the means by which to kill it. The prevailing attitudes of the time either considered wildlife purely for its sporting potential or as pests to be controlled. To view animals in the wild through anything but the crosshairs on a rifle seemed a faintly absurd, pointless proposition. Deer, game, fish, birds of prey and larger mammals were fair quarry to be hunted and killed; the wilder and rarer, the better.

Dissenters from this view were few and far between. There were the scientists and naturalists, of course, but also a small band of individuals who had begun using photography for the first time to capture wildlife scenes. Two brothers from Yorkshire – Richard and Cherry Kearton – were among the founding fathers of the new photographic discipline, and it was their work that was to influence Scotland's greatest wildlife photographer and writer.

By his teenage years, Seton Gordon was already a committed and skilled naturalist. Inspired by the Keartons, Gordon would roam Deeside and the Cairngorms tracking and photographing birds and their nesting sites. He became a published writer at the age of fifteen, and in 1907, at the age of twenty-one, had published his first book, *Birds of the Loch and the Mountain*.

A prolific series of publications were to follow over his long life: twenty-seven books in total, as well as many articles on all aspects of Scotland's natural history, people and folklore. Gordon's vast interest in and knowledge of Scotland's wildlife and landscape were unparalleled (and have ever yet to be matched) but it is the Cairngorms that he is perhaps most associated with and which appear most widely in his writing.

Gordon knew the Cairngorms intimately and wrote two books about the range. The first (and only his second published book), *The Charm of the Hills*, was written at the age of twenty-six and charted his early, but already hugely well-informed, interactions with the Cairngorms. The second, *The Cairngorm Hills of Scotland*, followed over a decade later and is a more accomplished literary piece, yet still brims with the kind of youthful enthusiasm that characterised his entire life's work.

It is hard to read either of the books and not be engaged by the spectacle of what Gordon experiences. Whether it is journeying through a ferocious blizzard, being caught in a forest fire or simply foraging for berries, Gordon depicts scenes with a tangible sense of reality. Even a mid-winter's woodland walk takes on a special significance in Gordon's writing.

A little way into the forest I saw ahead of me a flood of sunlight on the woodland path and in less than a minute I had left the mist behind me and was walking through a fairy-like country. Overhead the sky was a deep glorious blue and no single cloud floated on that wide arch ... Not the faintest air stirred in the forest that day: the ground was white with rime, each birch tree a delicate tracery of frost-encrusted branches.

Gordon's writing and photography pioneered an alternative perception of the natural history of the Cairngorms and Scotland. For the first time it became possible to feel metaphorically conveyed to the snow-covered wastes of the high plateau, to know the complex gyres of an eagle's flight pattern or to imagine yourself exploring a hidden corrie.

Few other people could have achieved such authentic descriptions of the Cairngorms. But Gordon was unique. He was singular not only in his knowledge of the range, but also of the people who lived there. Despite his privileged background, Gordon was befriended by many of the stalkers and keepers who worked in the Cairngorms, men he admired greatly and who shared their knowledge freely with him. 'The Highland stalker has a certain distinctive charm.' Gordon observed. 'He has lived out his quiet life in the glen with the big hills he knows so well . . . a stalker has more intimate knowledge of the ground than any other man'.

It was undoubtedly his collaboration with many estate workers that provided him with the vital information and assistance in gaining such close access to many of the nesting sites that he would meticulously observe. But Gordon was also fanatical in his observations, possessing, like MacGillivray, a seemingly insatiable curiosity for the natural world that overcame the hardships and dangers such a fascination entailed, especially in the Cairngorms.

This resolve is not readily noticed in Gordon's work, for much of his writing conveys a sense of understated fortitude, a matter-of-fact stoicism that makes it easy to look past the many cold hours spent in hides, the treacherous journeys to remote areas of the range or the perilous climbs to cliff-top eyries. Only occasionally are there glimpses of the adversity that Gordon must have encountered.

In one instance while he is photographing an eagle's nest, 'standing motionless for hours on a narrow ledge . . . not daring to move, in a bitter north wind and driving snow showers,' Gordon realises that he has become crag-fast with the cold and inactivity. 'I found that my legs had lost their power and that I was quite unable to descend the cliff. I stood there, perched high on the rock, with a curious feeling of helplessness until my wife . . . climbed up and guided my feet into the footholds while I made a painfully slow descent.'

A lifetime spent in the natural world also engendered an almost transcendental connection with it for Gordon. In one of his most spiritual accounts he retells the experience of night-walking across the Northern Corries, traversing the mountains before sunrise in what he called 'the season of dreams'.

At two o'clock I reached the summit of Cairngorm. A faint air drifted across from the south but even here, more than four thousand feet above the sea, the night air was not cold. The sky, all but the northern fringe, was now overspread by thin high cloud. In the light of dawn the snowy wastes of Ben MacDhui were pale and chill . . . I lay on dry lichen and heather beside a snowfield at the source of a hill burn and there waited for the strengthening day. The scene was one of outstanding beauty . . . The light strengthened and mysterious objects revealed themselves. In this world of grandeur the sky was at rest, the hills were at rest, one had the impression of infinite peace, the material and the spiritual worlds had joined hands.

At the time, no one else had written about Scotland's landscape in such comprehensive and revolutionary terms. And in doing so, Gordon initiated a quite radical change in public opinion. No longer were Scotland's wildlife and wild places the cultural and intellectual preserve of sportsmen and landowners. Gordon introduced natural history to the populace at large, so much so that it became an acceptable, even desirable, interest to aspire to.

Gordon's work was to inspire many, including a nine-year-old boy from Aberdeenshire who wrote to him in the autumn of 1939. The letter was simple and endearing, an enthused stream of youthful consciousness. 'I would like to go through the Lairig Ghru from Aviemore to Braemar,' the letter begins. 'I have never seen a golden eagle. I wear a kilt, I am getting your book, *The Cairngorm Hills of Scotland* for my birthday.' Across the page, in the middle of the letter are six separate boxes, each with a child's drawing of different scenes from the Cairngorms: a golden eagle; the Lairig Ghru; a deer; a lizard; a ptarmigan and a kilted stick-man figure walking in the mountains. 'I read your book *Afoot in Wild Places*, and I like the pictures, they were very nice . . . I would like to climb Lochnagar. I am nine years old. Do you think I will manage. I would be very happy if I could climb it.'

The letter must have moved Gordon, for he soon responded. 'I was very glad to see your nicely written letter and the interesting pictures you drew,' Gordon wrote. 'It is a fine thing for you to have a love of the hills,' he continued encouragingly, 'because on the hills you find yourself near grand and beautiful things, and as you grow older you will love them more and more.'

And so began a friendship that would span four decades and that would inspire the Cairngorm's most influential writer, climber and ecologist. 'Seton Gordon had an extraordinary effect on my life,' wrote Adam Watson about his friend and mentor. 'I do not understand why, and may never do so . . . It was as if an electric switch had been suddenly turned on in my head, so that now I saw the Cairngorms and the world in a new light.'

It was on a rainy day, during a family holiday to Ballater, that the young Watson had chanced upon a copy of the *The Cairngorm Hills of Scotland* in the local library. He was instantly captivated. 'Only perhaps once or twice in a lifetime may a brief event, such as glance at a book, or a sudden union of two minds, become a clear turning point which transforms the rest of one's life.' The effect on Watson was profound, his life's course determined thereafter by the discovery of that book. He went on to become the pre-eminent authority on the Cairngorms, spending a lifetime exploring the range. He traversed the mountains extensively on Nordic skis, studied rock ptarmigan on the high peaks, analysed snow patches in remote corries, seconded Tom Patey on the climbing-routes for the Cairngorm's first climbing guide and also wrote the SMC guidebook to the range. Watson never forgot the impact that Seton Gordon had on him, and he later dedicated his 1974 book, *The Cairngorms: Their Natural History and Scenery*, to his mentor, the man 'who lit the spark'.

Once inside Rothiemurchus, when you are deep within its boundaries, something soon becomes apparent. It becomes clear that the forest is not a place of continual enclosure, of unceasing overarching branches and under-growth as imagined from the outside. Unseen from its dense, tree-thick edges are large areas of open ground, enclosed and hidden within the wider perimeters of the forest. These spaces are occasionally surprising and vast, clearings that are stepped into without warning. It is then possible unexpectedly to find yourself in acreages of ozone and pasture, prairie-like fields distantly bordered by treelines and framed beyond that by mountains.

As I wandered, I had come to expect these interruptions to the forest and enjoyed their suddenness and incongruity. They were also ideal places to spot wildlife, transitional zones between the trees that both exposed and invited animals. In one such clearing I spotted a roe deer breaking from cover, springing in small, fast leaps like an antelope. Elsewhere I saw more birds, a small flock of crested tits, flying skittishly between solitary pines, black-and-white head-feathers quiffed like chequered cow-licks.

I walked through several of these moorland oases, each time breaking from the forest's submarine hues into a bright, tungsten light of sunshine and snow patches, eyes blinking. On each occasion I immediately scanned the open ground, hoping, but not expecting, to glimpse one of Britain's almost mythical creatures – the animal I most wanted to see in the wild, but which, ironically, I had the least chance of seeing.

The Scottish wildcat is even more elusive than the pine marten. Necessarily guarded in its habits, the wildcat's last strongholds in Britain are in the places where it can find greatest secrecy, namely the Scottish Highlands. The distribution across the Highlands is broad, with populations recorded in the far north as well as the west and the isles. There is also a significant wildcat presence, historically and currently, in the wild lands that border the Cairngorms.

Throughout my time in the Cairngorms, I had naively harboured thoughts of seeing a wildcat, of spotting the tiger-like markings, the muscular frame and thick, blunt-ended tail of the United Kingdom's only native feline. Unsurprisingly my path had never crossed with one of the country's most endangered and furtive mammals – or if it had, I had been none the wiser. But Rothiemurchus, and in particular its open spaces, are ideal wildcat territory. Here, amid the forestry and rocky outcrops, shelter and breeding grounds are close at hand, and so too are their favoured hunting grounds: moorland and water systems rich in prey and cover.

But sightings of wildcats are often fleeting and inconclusive, perhaps lasting only a few seconds or more. They become the stuff of anecdotes and tall tales. Stories are told of momentary glimpses – of a mysterious creature dissolving effortlessly back into its surroundings.

$\sim$

I found Loch an Eilein later that morning. It appeared as a silver band showing brightly through the thick screen of pines that crowded its banks. The surface was static and unreflective, resembling snow initially or the neutral blankness of an overcast sky. As I got closer, I could see the loch was almost entirely frozen, set fast in a glaucoma-grey crust, the cloudy colour of animal blindness. Near the shoreline woodland debris had become trapped in the ice, resembling botanical specimens in a display case: yellow birch leaves scattered like heart-shaped confetti and pine-cones suspended in the frozen water.

I walked the path that paralleled the five-kilometre perimeter of the loch. For hours I had been rambling in solitude, now I passed dozens of people: families with children charging around them like electrons, strolling couples, dog-walkers and lycra-clad cyclists. This was the Rothiemurchus of the tourist brochures and the Victorian day-trippers: the trinket loch overlooked by rugged hills with its hidden coves and small wooded island. But darker history exists here too.

The island at the north-western edge of the loch was once one of the strongholds of Alexander Stewart, the Earl of Buchan – better known as the Wolf of Badenoch, one of the most notorious characters of Highland history. Stewart had a fearsome reputation for cruelty and rapacity. His private army of cateran forces enforced a tyrannical rule over a vast area of northern Scotland stretching as far west as the Isles of Skye and Harris. The Wolf's propensity towards violence was renowned. Following a feud with the Bishop of Moray, Stewart sacked the village of Forres and later Elgin, razing its cathedral to the ground.

A fortification has stood on the tiny island since the early thirteenth century and the castle is still visible from the lochside today, the walls partially hidden under a creep of foliage with crows haggling above its ramparts. One of Scotland's last ospreys had once nested in the relative safety of the castle, before it was harried from the site by egg thieves in the early twentieth century. The birds became extinct in Britain shortly afterwards, but returned in the 1950s and successfully re-colonised parts of Scotland, in particular the nearby Loch Garten.

It is thought that the Loch an Eilein islet was once connected to the shoreline by a causeway. The walkway can no longer be seen, but is rumoured to be somewhere below the surface of the water, covered in the late eighteenth century when the construction of a sluice gate on the loch for timber felling raised the water level.

At the southernmost point of the loch, a small path cut left into more trees by a narrow burn. I followed the path, ducking under branches and stepping over tree-roots, emerging on the banks of another smaller loch, a quarter of the size of Loch an Eilein and narrower; only half a kilometre in length and a few hundred metres at its widest point.

Reaching Loch Gamhna felt like stepping into an ante-chamber, a smaller, discrete version of a larger, adjacent space. The views had opened up. I looked out across a large reed bed, the stalks frozen to nubs like crop stubble. On the other side of the loch I could see the rugged frontage of Kennapole Hill and the broken slopes of its two eastern-facing crags, Creag an Fhithich and Creag à Chait. I made my way to the crags the long way round, circling the loch on its narrow path. The place was quiet, devoid of the crowds of the larger loch and more serene. In summer, I had heard that water lilies grew here at the edge of the loch and I tried to imagine the place brimming with warmth and fecundity.

From the water's edge I moved up a scrubby incline covered in large tussocks of frozen grass. After five minutes of surprisingly hard work I was standing in grainy snow at the foot of the crags, panting hard. I surveyed the steep walls of white rock that curved the hillside above me. I could see two distinct buttresses, each about fifty feet high. In several places, trees had established themselves in between rocks on the cliff-face, thriving in positions inaccessible to deer. If the legends were true, it was here, somewhere among the tangram of fallen boulders, fissures and cracks that I would find the Cat's Den.

My search was haphazard. I moved from one dark recess to another. Each time I found a space that was, on closer inspection, either too small or too shallow to accommodate a human. After each thwarted discovery, I would spot another potential cave that would set my adrenalin coursing again. After an hour I had scoured most of the crags without success. All I had found was a small cleft under a ledge of rock, big enough to allow a cramped bivouac, but surely too insignificant to be considered a cave.

I thought back to my search for the El Alamein shelter and the difficulty of finding something so inscrutable in the landscape. I remembered also Henry Alexander's description of the Cat's Den: 'a cave not easily found, in the rocks on the face of Kennapole Hill', and I began to wonder if, without first-hand knowledge of its whereabouts, I would ever find it.

My last chance was to try the uppermost level of the cliffs. I clambered upwards, my bare fingers reddened by the snow and cold rock. Eventually I reached the point where I could climb no further without a rope and companions. I had not been able to get to the top of the crags, but there in a section of rock hidden behind the cliff-face, and therefore impossible to spot by standing square-on to the hill, was what I had been looking for. I knew straight away that I had found the Cat's Den.

The cave was neat and unassuming. It had been formed where blocks from the cliffs above had dropped onto the gap between two small buttresses, creating a roof of wedged boulders. The entrance was a black triangle, less than three feet wide and no more than four feet high. An old birch, its bark the same chalky white colour as the rocks, had at some point fallen onto the cave but had continued to grow, and now rested against its roof-blocks like a supporting spar, its limbs entwined with the granite.

I followed a line of rocks, covered in green moss, that made a small pathway to the cave's opening and stood outside for a moment. The interior was so dark that it was impossible to see what was there. I felt suddenly apprehensive about entering into the space, my head filled with thoughts of fugitives and a concern about the precarious weight above me. For some reason I held my breath as I went in, ducking my shoulders into the small gap as if diving underwater.

Once inside, I was able to stand upright and I let my eyes adjust to the gloom. The cave was not completely enclosed. A small gap, with plants growing round the outside, faced the entranceway, filtering in a greenish light. The space inside was small, but the roof sloped diagonally so it was possible to shuffle about at one end. And by lying with feet tucked in at the lowest section it was spacious enough to sleep in. It smelt woody – veg-etated, but not damp. There was no sign that the cave had been recently used or even visited, and I wondered who had been the last person to set foot in there.

I imagined Black Sandy living there. It must have been one of the Cairngorm's earliest howffs and it seemed the perfect hiding place; located deep within the forest and set high up in the crags, the cave was difficult to access and completely concealed from sight. Its height was also a vantage point, enabling any unwelcome visitors to be spotted a mile off. There was space to sleep, sit and even make a fire, all the time protected from the worst of the Cairngorm weather.

It was exhilarating to have found it. Perhaps, then, the legend of Black Sandy was true. If so, this cave was the reason that he had managed to evade capture. Without this place he may not have been able to make good his escape to America. And if the full extent of the story is to be believed and the course of history extrapolated, then without this cave, President Ulysses Grant – Black Sandy's supposed descendant – may have never been born.

Back outside, I squinted in the brighter light, curving my hand across my forehead like a visor. From the narrow ledge by the cave's entrance I could see for miles. I looked down on the two lochs and traced the route I had taken across the vast swathes of the deep-emerald forestry.

It was then that I saw them. Lower down, on one of the boulders which I had heaved myself up on, there were paw-prints. They were fresh, made only hours before my arrival and were perfectly cast in the granular snow. I moved closer to look at them.

There were a dozen or more, scattered in a line of best fit running diagonally across the boulder. They were roughly circular, and between 4–5cm in diameter. Each had a clearly defined central pad, with four smaller toe pads spread above it. I noticed that the direction of several of the prints was different, facing the opposite way, signalling an about-turn. I followed them down to a lower ledge, where I found many more prints, records of multiple movements, back and forth across the same area. They lacked the oblong shape of a fox and were too small to be a dog's. I immediately thought of pine martens, but I could find no sign of claws. Then it dawned on me. Of course, these were cat prints. Surely too far from habitation to be a domestic cat, they must be the tracks of a wildcat!

Suddenly it all made sense. The name of the place, Creag a' Chait, meant the Cat's Crag. I had always thought it referred to the human history, to Black Sandy and the Cat's Den. But what if the name predated the fugitive's story, referring instead to a natural history? Wildcats may have lived here for centuries, sheltering among the multitude of hidden crevices.

Perhaps that was how Sandy Grant had known about the crags. If he had hunted wildcats here, he would have known of its potential for hiding places. Or maybe finding his den had been intuitive: linking the wildcats' preference for secrecy and cover with the possibility for human shelter in the remote rocky outcrop. I liked that. The sense that these secret histories could be transferred through the landscape, passed on through time by word of mouth or more recently by a place name written on a map.

Ravine

'I have discovered my mountain – its weathers, its airs and lights, its singing burns, its haunted dells, its pinnacles and tarns, its birds and flowers, its long blue distances.'

Nan Shepherd, *The Living Mountain*.

It had been over two years since I walked to the source of the Dee. The journeys which I had initially thought would take a few seasons to complete had required much longer. I had been sidetracked and sidelined; caught up in the demands of everyday life and held back in the city during a couple of exceptionally cold winters.

Now, though, there was only one more secret history in the Cairngorms left for me to find, at least for the time being anyway. As on my first journey, I would be following another river: the Water of Ailnack, one of the many tendrils of the River Avon. I liked the idea of ending my journeys by walking the route of another water course; it seemed fitting and gave symmetry to my time in the range. There was also an obvious association between rivers and secrecy.

Water finds the lowest point in a landscape, sometimes inside a landscape. Where geology permits, often in karst areas of carbonate rock – limestone, gypsum, dolomite – water can slip from view, disappearing through sinkholes and forming subterranean waterways, both hidden and secret. The Cairngorms has such invisible waters. There is the March Burn that flows off the west side of Ben Macdui; its downward progress can be tracked from the plateau until it vanishes at an elevation of around 900 metres before surfacing again in the Pools of Dee. The Wells of Dee were equally enigmatic, reaching fresh air as an established stream channelled directly from some mysterious underground reservoir.

Entry and exit points of subterrestrial waters are often places of numinous significance. Since pre-Christian times, 'cloutie wells' have held a spiritual and superstitious importance. To this day, votive offerings are made at the sites of these springs, traditionally by hanging a rag on a nearby 'cloutie tree'. At one such well, near Munlochy in the Black Isle, hundreds of cloths adorn the trees and bushes nearby, hanging like prayer flags or Christmas-tree decorations.

Water also carves into a landscape, gradually eating away at the bedrock, gorging and gorge-making. The effects of this erosion process can be spectacular. Ravines are created that can seem impossibly deep and near-vertical in their declivities. There were several such places that I knew of in Scotland – the Black Rock Gorge in Easter Ross and Dollar Glen in Clackmannanshire – and I considered them to be the some of the most daunting and stunning geological features I had ever come across. I had heard that parts of the Water of Ailnack possessed similar qualities and my maps appeared to confirm this. They also showed a sudden convergence of contour lines at the far end of the Water that I planned to head to, a place referred to mysteriously as the Castle.

———

What was immediately obvious was that the Water of Ailnack was not immediately obvious. I had made my way south-west from the village of Tomintoul and was walking in the high moorland that flanked the river. Indigo clouds massed to the south, and a warm wind hinted at thunder. I passed a greenshank flying repetitive circuits, landing then returning to the air, its call a shrill *kew kew*.

I was less than 300 metres from the Water, yet it was impossible to see where it ran. It was there somewhere, embedded in the wide cleft that split the otherwise unbroken plateau of grass and heather. From further away even this feature would be lost. The landscape would appear continuous at eye level, the Water and its gully completely invisible.

On first impression this seemed like barren country. The distance between my feet and the horizon consisted of nothing but kilometres of tawny moor. And for a while I had the strange feeling of walking in a desert, somewhere featureless and immeasurable. Viewed carefully, though, the place took on a different perspective. With every few hundred metres I began to notice differences in the natural configurations of the moor. Heather gave way to grasses: deer, soft rush and sedge, which ceded in their turn to territories of moss that were then replaced by larger shrubs, gorse and bog myrtle. I spotted other smaller plants too, tormentil, blaeberry and cloudberry.

Far from being an expanse of uniformity, the moorland was constantly varying and full of colour. I came across bright yellow in the starfish leaves of butterwort, rhubarb-pink in the tentacles of sundew and snow white in the flowering heads of bog cotton. Up until the early part of the last century, this botanical diversity would have been crucially important to the lives of people in and around the Cairngorms. Previous inhabitants of the range would have been intimately familiar with the plants, both for their practical uses and superstitious significance.

Heather was used for a multitude of applications, including basket-making, thatching, bedding, for cordage and as a dye. It could even be used as a remedy for coughs as well as for making ale. Another of the most ubiquitous plants of the range has also been used for centuries. Sphagnum moss's absorbency and natural concentrations of iodine have meant it is ideal for use as a sterile dressing for wounds. It was supposedly used to staunch the injuries of Scottish soldiers after the battle of Flodden, and was collected in industrial quantities from the Highlands for use during the First and Second World Wars.

Almost every species of plant would have been valued for a particular function. The roots of the flower tormentil were prized for tanning leather and as a cure for diarrhoea. Juniper was burnt in houses so that its acrid smoke would cleanse the home of pests. The shoots of soft rushes, when peeled, dried and soaked in animal fat, would serve as slow-burning candles. Bog myrtle was also highly useful as a fever-remedy, a cure for ulcers and a natural insect repellent. To this day, hill-goers often rub the crushed leaves of bog myrtle on their skin to ward off midges. Spiritual associations were also intensely valued. Clubmoss and butterwort were considered lucky and carried as charms, especially when travelling, whereas plants such as foxglove were linked with witchcraft.

Awareness of this plant lore has been all but lost in modern-day lives, but occasional fragments of this ancestral knowledge remain. They survive in contemporary customs and habits: brambles collected in autumn, mistletoe and holly brought into homes at Christmas and rowan trees planted outside houses to ward off evil spirits.

The triangulated connection between the humans, plants and mountains of the Cairngorms was keenly observed by Nan Shepherd. The 'living things', she believed, were impossible to separate from 'the forces that create them, for the mountain is one and indivisible, and rock, soil, water and air are no more integral to it than what grows from the soil and breathes air.'

Shepherd saw this interaction between plant and human life and the Cairngorms as not only mutually beneficial, but vital. 'Heather grows in its most profuse luxuriance on granite, so that the very substance of the mountain is in its life'. In doing so the roots of the plants fulfil a reciprocal purpose, binding the soil and holding fast the fabric of the mountain and the human life it sustains. This interconnectedness was central to Shepherd's unifying and radical view of the Cairngorms. It was a proposition that viewed every part of the range as 'aspects of one entity', the eponymous 'living mountain' of her short but beguiling thought-piece book.

The Living Mountain was written in the 'disturbed and uncertain world' that existed in the latter years of the Second World War, and was a kind of meditative sanctuary for Shepherd. She described it as 'a secret place of ease', where she recalled memories of Cairngorm ventures many years afterwards. At the time of completion just after the war, one publisher was approached to take the book, but the manuscript was courteously rejected and spent the following thirty years stuffed in a drawer and forgotten about until its eventual publication in 1977. The book, though, is exceptional, and its concept remains ground-breaking even by contemporary standards: it is a physical, emotional and sensory character-study of a single range of mountains, a British mountain monograph quite unlike anything that has been written before or since.

Mountaineering and mountain literature have traditionally tended towards the prosaic, an evolution, partly, of the old climbing-club journals and their instructional approach to route-finding and wayfaring. In pre-modern mountain literature, where wonderment with the landscape occurs, as it did with MacGillivray and Seton Gordon, the appreciation is no less valid but is often a by-product of some other reason for being there. *The Living Mountain* is different. It is a book written in retrospect, a consigning to paper of many years of Cairngorm exploration that occurred for no other purpose than to satisfy a deep and continuing personal fascination. It was a captivation that for Shepherd, seemed inexhaustible. 'However often I walk on them,' Shepherd wrote, 'these hills hold astonishment for me. There is no getting accustomed to them.'

Shepherd's interactions with the Cairngorms were indeed vast – full-bodied connections with every aspect of their environment. She describes seeing the plateau 'glittering white . . . an immaculate vision, sun-struck, lifting against a sky of dazzling blue'. Elsewhere, she notices minute details. 'If one can look below the covering ice on a frozen burn, a lovely pattern of indentations is found, arched and chiselled, the obverse of the water's surface.'

What is so unusual about the book is that explorations are recalled that are multi-sensory, not just visual. Descriptions of the mountains include the sounds of storms, of gales crashing into corries, of cloudbursts roaring in the ravines and thunder that 'reverberates with a prolonged and menacing roll'. There are smells everywhere too, fragrances that are 'aromatic and heady', like the scent of heather and pine released by the sun, or the brandy-like perfume of birch when it rains. Elsewhere, she finds 'spicy juniper' and 'honey-sweet orchids', even the 'earthy smell of moss', the 'rank smell of deer' or the 'sharp scent of fire'. 'I draw life in through the delicate hairs of my nostrils,' Shepherd wrote.

'Touch,' Shepherd remarks, 'is the most intimate sense of all,' from the sensory pleasure she finds walking barefoot through heather to the feel of rainwater on juniper when brushed against the hand, the 'wet drops trickling over the palm', or the way cold spring water tingles the throat, wind flattens the cheeks, frost stiffens muscles and cold air makes 'lungs crackle'. Taste is another sense she evokes, in the 'subtle and sweet' flavours of cloudberries and blaeberries.

Shepherd's focus on the sensual response to her explorations of the mountains forms the basis of an almost metaphysical appreciation of the Cairngorms. Once there, she writes, 'the eye sees what it didn't see before, or sees in a new way what it had already seen. So the ear, the other senses. It is an experience that grows . . . unpredictable and unforgettable, come the hours when heaven and earth fall away and one sees a new creation'. No other British mountain range can claim such a spiritualised, philosophical discourse. The Lakes had their Romantic devotees, in particular Coleridge and Wordsworth, but nothing they wrote approaches the collective focus Shepherd brings to bear in *The Living Mountain*.

Few other writers can rival such exclusivity of concentration on one particular place, especially a mountain range. Shepherd knew the Cairngorms intimately, almost confidentially. She contoured as much as she climbed; she lingered, meandered, waited and observed, eschewing the typical linear routes to summits, searching instead for the range's 'hidden recesses'. 'Often the mountain gives itself most completely when I have no destination,' Shepherd observed, 'where I reach nowhere in particular, but have gone out merely to be with the mountains as one visits a friend.' Over time, and seen through the assemblage of her memories in *The Living Mountain*, Shepherd's journeys become a kind of lens. A way of viewing the many inter-linking narratives she encounters in the range, gathered together as one indivisible form, the all-encompassing identity of the Cairngorms that she refers to ardently and collectively as 'the total mountain'.

The Water of Ailnack was well hidden. From the edge of the ravine I caught glimpses of it in small segments, bright pulses of surface light, showing 100 feet or more below me. Occasionally I would be able to stand directly above it, peering vertically down into glassy black water that faded to clear, shallow amber.

At the midpoint of the ravine, where a small tree-covered burn flowed in from the west, I dropped down to the water's edge. The river was low and I managed to clamber along the banks for a while, clinging to handfuls of heather as I moved through the bottom of the gorge. I imagined the place during stormy weather. Rainwater would pour in from the Water's source high on the mountainside of Bynack More, and from all around the surrounding moor-land. There was literally nowhere else for the water to go. It would funnel into the ravine with incredible ferocity, carving a passage deeper into the landscape. There would be little chance of escape if the Water was to rise. Sud-denly, the place felt darkly submerged; sunk down below the world of plateau and moor, an emphatic contradiction of the Cairngorm's limitless horizons.

Ravine

With thoughts of thunderheads and flash floods, I moved back to higher ground. From above, the slopes into the ravine looked more precipitous than before. Outcrops of rock protruded high above the river and steep landslides of loose grit and stone looked poised to slip at any moment. On several of these scree-runs I spotted horizontal tracks that contoured hundreds of feet above the Water. Remarkably, sheep must have made their way across this perilously unfastened terrain with some regularity.

I walked across several more kilometres of blank moorland, and then saw something completely unexpected. Below me, as the ravine deepened and curved in a tight S-bend, it had become filled with trees. It was a small wood, perhaps fifty or sixty trees in total, completely unmarked on the map and hidden from the upper surface of the moor. Some of the trees looked ancient: long-lived birch and willow with bushy crowns of mint-green leaves. Elsewhere, saplings were growing at the margins, small scrawny specimens clinging to the most improbable of inclines; the wood was regenerating itself. Unlike so many areas of forestry in the Cairngorms these trees were expanding, colonising somewhere neither humans, sheep nor deer would actively reach. It was one of the most astounding sights I had come across in the range, a thriving secret landscape, anomalous and cartographically unnoticed.

Within half an hour, I had arrived at the Castle. I had been walking for several hours, although the distance felt much longer. The feature was unmistakeable. It was a place contained within the landscape, made unique by its confines and restrictions. It was a downward world, defined by its inward limits rather than outward expanses. The Water made a sharp bend below me, turning ninety

173

degrees before it narrowed to a thin channel that ran beneath two large cliffs. The gap formed a window in the landscape, and in the distance, I could see a layering of blue-grey hills fading away to the south.

This was the deepest part of the Ailnack gorge: from the uppermost level of the moor the drop was perhaps ta hundred metres to the water below. On the western side of the ravine, there were two huge landslips. The largest formed a gash running almost the entire height of the slope. Soil and vegetation had been recently stripped from the surface, leaving behind a laceration of flesh-pink earth. I had read that the geology here was different from the rest of the range. The ravine sat within a small area of old red sandstone, formed from rock that had been eroded from the Caledonian Mountains over four hundred million years ago.

I wondered at the name of the place, and who had thought of it. The Castle seemed a strange choice. There appeared to be no sign of an actual fortification. Perhaps the cliffs had suggested imaginary battlements, or the gorge a moat, but I struggled to make the connection. Maybe the name was more metaphorical, indicating something guarded or guarding, the entranceway or exit from the mountains, somewhere prone to violent transactions of power.

As I turned to leave, a peregrine dropped down from cliffs on the opposite side of the gorge. I had never seen one so close, the sleek, fish-like body and the narrow angle-bracket wings. It curved round near to where I walked and flew behind me, rising with a high-pitched call, before swooping in the same wide circle again and again. I was being told to leave, warned off by the Castle's sentry.

Conventional cartography struggles with gorges and ravines, as it does with cliffs and any extreme steepness. The plan-view can never satisfactorily describe the vertical plane because it assumes the same view – looking straight down. Orthographic projection in this sense is limited, capturing the three-dimensional with only a partial likeness. Although a notion of the visual reality can be gained, the drama and scale of precipitous landscapes are rarely accurately imagined from such a map. It was for this reason that I almost completely missed the most spectacular part of the Ailnack Ravine.

Near where I had begun the walk, a couple of kilometres into the moor, I noticed a wooden post, rooted in the ground at an angle. Curious as to its purpose, I left the track I was on to inspect it. Either deliberately, or coincidentally, the post marked the ravine's most outstanding viewpoint. I looked down onto rapids. The Water had now widened and whitened, blockaded by large boulders that from a distance looked like stepping stones. Here, downstream, the ravine had changed in size and appearance. It was much bigger and filled by huge rock walls dotted with matchstick conifers, pines and larch. It resembled a frontier landscape, the backdrop to a Western, a North American not Scottish scene, a canyon not a ravine. There had been nothing on the map to suggest somewhere with such visual impact; it was another secret landscape, hidden in plain sight.

I scanned the cliffs as they dropped towards the Water, trying with difficultly to gauge their scale. The walls were full of texture, and as I looked closely I could make out a pattern: a horizontal banding occurring at various heights, gradations in the rocks at perfect parallels to each other. These were markers, water-lines etched into the rock at successively lower levels indicating the river's gradual and continuing progression into the land. I was looking at the multi-million year history of the ravine's downward journey, a chronological plimsoll-line measuring the barely comprehensible stages of its descent.

—

The next day I woke early and dismantled my tent in the quickening half-light, keen to make one last walk before I headed home. I moved through forestry thick with mist, Rothiemurchus, then Glenmore, before heading north and gaining height above the trees. By early morning, I was at the top of Meall a' Bhuachaille, the largest hill on a small ridge that sits ten kilometres to the north of the Northern Corries.

The summit was marked by a large cairn. From either side of the stone pile, rocks had been extended in each direction, curving around in two drystone arms to form an incomplete circle, resembling a sheep-fold or an iron-age broch. I sat outside the shelter, my face exposed to the wind, and looking south, I mapped the visible portions of the range.

It started to my left, from the steep slopes that banked above the mysterious Lochan Uaine, in whose waters an aquamarine light is perpetually suspended. Then the land rose, stretching in a long and gradual ridgeline past Stac na h-Iolaire – the Eagle's Crag – and on to Cnap Coire na Spreidhe, near where I had found the El Alamein refuge. I counted out and named the Northern Corries: the deserted Coire Laogh Mór; Coire na Ciste and Coire Cas, the ski corries; and Coire an t-Sneachda and Coire an Lochan, whose huge rock walls were still streaked with last winter's snow. The plateau continued further east, past the narrow gateway of the Chalamain Gap and beyond the space left by the glacial defile of the Lairig Ghru, to the distant summit of Braeriach, where I had spent the cold and moonlit night over two years ago. I could see, too, the point at which the Cairngorms ended, finishing so abruptly that the neatly defined bulk of the massif took the appearance of an island rising above the lower ground.

There was still so much more of the range that was beyond my present view. In my mind I went south to the cloistered interior of the mountains, to Loch Avon and the Shelter Stone, and to the west, to the tranquillity of Glen Feshie. In the east, I pictured the Fairy Glen with its secret howff, the vast tablelands of Beinn a' Bhuird and the surreal landscape of Ben Avon.

To view the entirety of the Cairngorms at ground-level is impossible, its boundaries are too vast and its recesses too intricate. No one place can provide such a single, all-encompassing perspective. The history of the range is much the same. There is no omniscient viewpoint, nothing emblematic that can condense or codify the many narratives of the range. Instead they are fragmented and multiple: individual stories, or more precisely individuals' stories.

Many are dark – tales of tragedy and misfortune, the traces of which are occasionally found in the landscape. Spectral reminders such as the deserted villages of Glen Dee or the aircraft wrecks scattered across the peaks. They are there without formal markers, remaining in the accounts of loved ones lost, of accidents and avalanches, of mistakes and misadventures. And they are there also in the ghosts of the Clearances.

But the Cairngorms have also been a place of refuge. For some, like Black Sandy evading the hue and cry or Peter Grant eluding capture by the Hanoverian government, its wildness offered the means of escape, enabled disappearance and anonymity. For others it represented a different kind of sanctuary. Nan Shepherd's meditative wanderings had led her to a state of transcendental companionship with the mountains, a quasi-spiritual interaction with what she reverentially described as the 'elementals'. The Duchess of Bedford had also found a similar affinity with the Cairngorm landscape, an idealised notion of the wild that nonetheless gave solace through its beauty and solitude. It was a sentiment shared and expounded in visual form by her lover Edwin Landseer, who had been simultaneously inspired and becalmed by the place.

Many others before and since have made similar connections. I thought of the early explorers, John Hill Burton and the Reverend George Skene Keith, plodding enthusiastically across the summits clutching barometers and notebooks, or the naturalists, William MacGillivray, Seton Gordon and Adam Watson, snowbound and shivering as they observed their quarry, or the pioneer climbers bedecked in tweed, fearlessly charting the vertical realms with nothing more than hawser ropes and alpenstocks.

The same was true, of course, for anyone whose ventures in the Cairngorms had in some way left them moved by the place. For most, these experiences have been unarticulated or unrecorded, at least in any official sense, although the markers of these individual passages remain: scribbles left in a bothy's visitors book; crampon marks etched on a rockface and place-names bequeathed by familiarity or admiration. But they are also recorded imaginatively, held in a collective consciousness, passed on by word of mouth, secret histories kept alive, told and retold, eventually passing into myth.

After a while I left the summit and descended east, my eyes streaming in the wind. I followed footprints made the day before, stepping into their rain-filled impressions and aligning my feet in the direction they had taken. Below me, several hundred metres in the vertical distance, I could see Ryvoan Bothy, its tiny shape brightly outlined in the landscape, sitting snugly in swells of moorland as if floating on a turbulent sea.

Acknowledgements

Much of the research for this book has been gathered from some superb secondary sources, including among others, celebrated books by Seton Gordon and Nan Shepherd. However, several invaluable points of reference have been taken from less well-known works that themselves play an equally important part in documenting the traditions, culture and history of the region. These include Ian Murray's fine books on the Deeside and the Cairngorms, as well as the indispensable Scottish Mountaineering Club district guides written by Henry Alexander and latterly by Adam Watson, which in their multi-decade span offer a unique insight into many of the most secretive features of the range. Likewise, Greg Strange's immense 100-year climbing history of the Cairngorms is an amazing archive of the Cairngorms' recreational history. Although covering other Scottish mountains in addition to the Cairngorms, I.D.S. Thomson's books *The Black Cloud* and *May the Fire Be Always Lit*, as well as Dave Brown and Ian Mitchell's *Mountain Days and Bothy Nights* draw on some evocative personal recollections and primary evidence which added a significant dimension to topics mentioned in the book. The *Cairngorm Club Journal* has also been a vital trove of information. I am grateful also to information about the Oxford aircrash provided by Linzee Duncan, both directly and indirectly, through her superb website, *www.archieraf.co.uk*, and to Ronald Turnbull for his initial correspondence.

Finally, thanks to my wife, Jacqui, for all her patience and support.

References and Sources

Aikman, Christian (ed.), Livingstone, Alastair (ed.), and Stuart Hart, Betty (ed.). (second edition 2001). *No Quarter Given: The Muster Roll of Prince Charles Edward Stuart's Army, 1745-46*. Neil Wilson Publishing.

Alexander, Sir Henry (first edition 1928, fourth edition 1968). *The Cairngorms*. Scottish Mountaineering Club District Guide. The Scottish Mountaineering Trust.

Allen, John (2010). *Cairngorm John*. Sandstone Press.

Bain, Clifton (2013). *The Ancient Pinewoods of Scotland*. Sandstone Press.

Barford, J. E. Q. (1946). *Climbing in Britain*. Pelican Books.

Barton, Bob and Wright, Blyth (second ed. 2000). *A Chance in a Million? Scottish Avalanches*. Scottish Mountaineering Trust.

Bennet, Donald (ed.) (third ed. 1999). *The Munros*. Scottish Mountaineering Trust.

Bolognesi, Robert (2007). *Avalanche! Understand and Reduce Risks from Avalanches*. Cicerone Press.

Bolognesi, Robert (2007). *Snow: Understanding, Testing and Interpreting Snow Conditions to Make Better Avalanche Predictions*. Cicerone Press.

Borthwick, Alastair (1939). *Always a Little Further*. Faber.

Brooker, W.D. (1988). *A Century of Scottish Mountaineering: An Anthology from the Scottish Mountaineering Club Journal*. Scottish Mountaineering Trust.

Brown, Dave and Mitchell, Ian (1987). *Mountain Days and Bothy Nights*. Luath Press.

Brown, Hamish (1980). *Hamish's Mountain Walk*. Paladin.

Brown, Hamish (2005). *Seton Gordon's Scotland: An Anthology*. Whittles Publishing.

Card, Frank (1993). *Whensoever: 50 Years of the RAF Mountain Rescue Service 1943-1993: 50 Years of RAF Mountain Rescue*. Ernest Press.

Cawthorne, Mike (2007). *Wilderness Dreams: The Call of Scotland's Last Wild Places*. In Pinn.

Connor, Jeff (1999). *Creag Dhu Climber: The Life and Times of John Cunningham*. Ernest Press.

Deakin, Roger (2008). *Wildwood: A Journey through Trees*. Penguin.

Defoe, Daniel (reprint edition 1978). *A Tour Through the Whole Island of Great Britain*. Penguin Classics.

Dickens, Charles (1879). *The Life of Charles James Mathews, chiefly autobiographical, with selections from his correspondence and speeches*. Macmillan and Co.

Drummond, Peter (Second ed. 2007). *Scottish Hill Names: Their Origin and Meaning*. Scottish Mountaineering Trust.

Duff, David (ed.) (1983). *Queen Victoria's Highland Journals*. Webb & Bower.

Duff, John (Second edition 2008). *A Bobby on Ben Macdhui: Life and Death on the Braes o' Mar*. Leopard Magazine Publishing.

Dunlop, Basil M. S (2005). *Cairngorm Stones: the Natural and Cultural History of Cairngorm Gemstones*. Grantown Museum and Heritage Trust.

Eliot, T. S., *The Waste Land* (1922).

Else, Richard and McNeish, Cameron (1994). *The Edge: One Hundred Years of Scottish Mountaineering*. BBC Books.

Fyffe, Allen and Nisbet, Andrew (Fourth ed. 1995). *The Cairngorms: Rock and Ice Climbs*, Vol.1. Scottish Mountaineering Trust.

Geiger, John (2010). *The Third Man Factor*. Canongate Books.

Gordon, Seton (1907). *Birds of the Loch and Mountain*. Cassell and Company.

Gordon, Seton (1912). *The Charm of the Hills*. Cassell and Company.

Gordon, Seton (1925). *The Cairngorm Hills of Scotland*. Cassell and Company.

Gordon, Seton (1937). *Afoot in Wild Places*. Cassell and Company.

Gordon, Seton (1951). *Highlands of Scotland*. Hale.

Grant, Elizabeth (new edition 2006). *Memoirs of a Highland Lady 1797-1827*. Canongate Books.

Gray, Affleck (1987). *Legends of the Cairngorms*. Mainstream Publishing.

Gray, Affleck (second Ed. 1994). *The Big Grey Man of Ben MacDhui*. Birlinn.

Gunn, Neil M. (1937). *Highland River*. The Porpoise Press.

Heaney, Seamus. 'Bogland'.

Hill Burton, John (1864). *The Cairngorm Mountains*. William Blackwood and Sons.

Knowlton, Derrick (1974). *The Naturalist in Scotland*. David & Charles.

Langmuir, Eric (third edition 1995). *Mountaincraft and Leadership*. SportScotland.

MacGillivray, William (1855). *The Natural History of Dee Side and Braemar*. Printed for private circulation [by Bradbury and Evans].

MacGillivray, William (1998). *A Walk to London*. Acair Ltd.

MacInnes, Hamish (third ed. 1998). *International Mountain Rescue Handbook*. Constable and Robinson.

Macmillan, Hugh (1907). *Rothiemurchus*. J. M. Dent.

Marshall, Meryl M. (2005). *Glen Feshie: The History and Archaeology of a Highland Glen*. North of Scotland Archaeological Society.

Maslen-Jones, Bob (1999). *A Perilous Playground: Misadventures in Snowdonia and the Development of the Mountain Rescue Services 1805-1990s*. Bridge Books.

McConnochie, A. I. (1907). *Guide to Aviemore and Vicinity*. J. S. Lawrence, Post Office.

McEwen, Lindsey J. and Werritty, Alan (2007). '"The Muckle Spate of 1829": the physical and societal impact of a catastrophic flood on the River Findhorn, Scottish Highlands.' Trans Inst Br Geogr, volume 32, pp. 66–89.

McKirdy Alan (ed.) (1995). *Cairngorms: A Landscape Fashioned by Geology*. Scottish Natural Heritage/British Geological Survey.

Mitchell, Ian (1998). *Scotland's Mountains before the Mountaineers*. Luath Press.

Moffat, Alistair (2010). *The Highland Clans*. Thames and Hudson Ltd.

Murray, Ian (1999). *Dee from the Far Cairngorms: Folklore and History from the Glens of Royal Deeside*. Lochnagar Publications.

Murray, Ian (2010). *The Cairngorms and Their Folk*. Lochnagar Publications.

Murray, Sheila (1987). *The Cairngorm Club 1887–1987*. The Cairngorm Club.

Murray, W.H. (1947). *Mountaineering in Scotland*. J.M. Dent and Sons Ltd.

Murray, W.H. (1951). *Undiscovered Scotland*. J.M. Dent and Sons Ltd.

Naismith, W. W. (1893). *Snowcraft in Scotland*. Scottish Mountaineering Club.

Nethersole-Thompson, Desmond and Watson, Adam (1974). *The Cairngorms: Their Natural History and Scenery*. Collins.

Nimlin, Jock (1980). *Let's Look at Scottish Gemstones*. Jarrold & Sons Ltd.

Nimlin, John (1948). 'Mountain Howffs'. *Scottish Mountaineering Club Journal*. Vol. XXIV.

Nimlin, John (1963). 'May the Fire Always Be Lit'. *Scottish Mountaineering Club Journal*. Vol. XXVII.

Ormond, Richard (2005). *The Monarch of the Glen: Landseer in the Highlands*. National Galleries of Scotland.

Patey, Tom (1962). 'Cairngorm Commentary'. *Scottish Mountaineering Club Journal*. Vol. XXVII.

Patey, Tom (Reprint edition 1986). *One Man's Mountains*. Gollancz.

Pennant, Thomas (2000). *A Tour in Scotland 1769*. Birlinn.

Perrin, Jim (1993). *Menlove: Life of John Menlove Edwards*. Ernest Press.

Prebble, John (1982). *The Highland Clearances*. Penguin.

Ralph, Robert (1999). *William MacGillivray: Creatures of Air, Land and Sea*. Merrell Publishers Ltd.

Scroggie, Sydney (1989). *The Cairngorms Scene and Unseen*. Scottish Mountaineering Trust.

Shackleton, Ernest (1919). *South: The Endurance Expedition*. Penguin.

Sharp, Bob and Whiteside, Judy (2005). *Mountain Rescue*. Hayloft Publishing.

Shepherd, Nan (1977). *The Living Mountain*. Aberdeen University Press.

Strange, Greg (2010). *The Cairngorms: 100 years of Mountaineering*. Scottish Mountaineering Trust.

Tewnion, A. (1958). 'A shot in the mist'. *The Scots Magazine*. June issue, 226-227.

The Statistical Account of Scotland (1791–1799).

Thompson, Francis (1979). *Portrait of the Spey*. Robert Hale Limited.

Thompson, Simon (2010). *Unjustifiable Risk? The Story of British Climbing*. Cicerone Press.

Thomson, I.D.S. (1993). *The Black Cloud*. Ernest Press.

Thomson, I.D.S. (1995). *May the Fire Be Always Lit: A Biography of Jock Nimlin*. Ernest Press.

Thoreau, Henry David (1854). *Walden*.

Trethewey, Rachel (2002). *Mistress of the Arts*. Review.

Turnbull, Ronald (2005). *Walking in the Cairngorms*. Cicerone Press.

Turnbull, Ronald (2007). *The Life and Times of the Black Pig: A Biography of Ben Macdui*. Millrace.

Turnbull, Ronald (2011). *Granite and Grit: A Walker's*

Guide to the Geology of British Mountains. Francis Lincoln.

Watson, Adam (1975). *The Cairngorms*. Scottish Mountaineering Club District Guide. The Scottish Mountaineering Trust.

Watson, Adam (2011). *It's a Fine Day for the Hill*. Paragon Publishing.

Watson, Adam (fifth edition 1975, sixth edition 1992). *The Cairngorms: Scottish Mountaineering Club District Guide*. Scottish Mountaineering Club.

Watson, Adam; Duncan, David and Pottie, John (2007). 'No Scottish snow survives until winter 2006/07'. *Weather*, volume 63 pp.71-73.

Wolfgang von Goethe, Johann (1828). *Faust, Part I*. Penguin Classics.

Worster, Donald (2008). *A Passion for Nature: The Life of John Muir*. Oxford University Press.

Wrightham, Mark (ed.), Kempe, Nick (ed.) (2006). *Hostile Habitats – Scotland's Mountain Environment: A Hillwalkers' Guide to Wildlife and the Landscape*. Scottish Mountaineering Trust.

Yeats, W. B., 'An Irish Airman Foresees His Death'.